ARGUNOMICS

The art of winning arguments

in the real world

Christopher H Hawkes

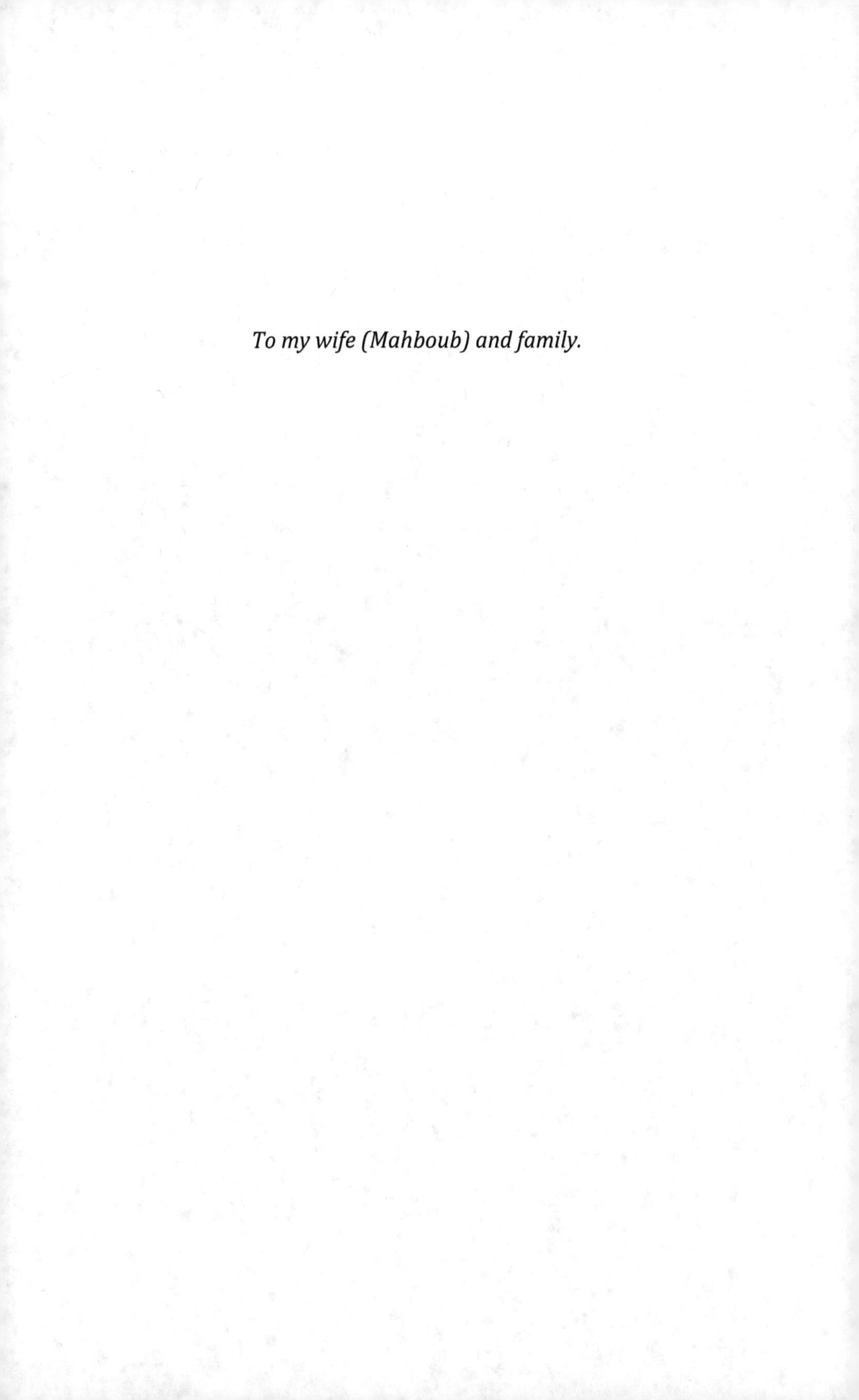

To my wife (Mahboub) and family.

CONTENTS

ACKNOWLEDGEMENTS

i

The author would like to express his thanks to Clive Goddard, cartoonist for Private Eye (amongst many other publications) and Chairman of the UK Professional Cartoonist's Organisation, for his drawings and ideas to help liven up relatively dry subject areas. To Professor Gary Cutter (University of Alabama, USA) for help with the statistics chapter. To Lydia Tyler (Magdalen College, Oxford) for her assistance with style and proof reading. To Martin Hawkes, my eldest son, for proof reading and helpful suggestions. Finally, to my wife and family for their tolerance and support while writing this book over the past 3 years.

Christopher H Hawkes

November 2024

INTRODUCTION

There are relatively few books written on the topic of debating. Many are written by academics and based on pure logic, making for dull reading. They often describe methods that would be difficult to apply in the real world. My book attempts address this drawback by clear explanation of techniques used in arguments and, it focuses on statistics, a subject that most people grasp poorly or prefer to dismiss as unreliable. I am frequently dismayed at the generally poor level of debate exhibited by politicians and media interviewers. Rarely is a question answered or if so, only after side-stepping the point with irrelevancies.

Debating can be fun. Many view this as a sport where the goal is to win. There are rather loosely defined rules for debating thus all means foul and fair are applied with the ultimate aim of victory. The purest form of debate is where each side is attempting to find the truth rather than humiliate their opponent or demonstrate their intellectual superiority. Search for the truth happens mostly between close friends or work colleagues, and even that runs the risk of harming a good relationship. Paradoxically, as proposed by Schopenhauer in the 19th century, when truth is discovered, it passes through three previous predictable stages: ridicule and denial; violent opposition and finally, acceptance as self-evident. For example, during research into duodenal ulcers during the 1950s, there were several descriptions of bacteria in the human stomach wall or its secretions. Most considered them to be co-incidental. Subsequently, two Australian scientists, Robin Warren and Barry Marshall demonstrated that a bacterium called Helicobacter Pylori was responsible for gastric and duodenal ulcers. Despite their observations, they were ridiculed at medical scientific meetings. In desperation, Dr Marshall swallowed gastric secretions from a patient with duodenal ulcer, and after a few days became ill with severe gastritis which would have progressed to duodenal ulcers! Eventually, their findings were accepted worldwide, and for their discovery they were awarded the Nobel Prize in 2005.

The ancient Greeks (Socrates, Cicero, Plato) defined the principles of reasoned debate but in the environment of politics, law, business, tribunals etc. they are applied infrequently. A popular approach favoured by philosophers is the so-called 'thought experiment', a pseudo-scientific term for trying to understand the consequences of a particular action - for example – 'what would be the effect of banning motor vehicles in the centre of London?' or 'what would be the effect in the UK of re-introducing the death penalty for treason / first degree murder etc'. This tactic tends to annoy scientists many of whom regard this as outdated. It is fine for identifying areas of ignorance, but scientists would argue that the only valid approach is to design an experiment, put it into practice and see what the result tells you. Rarely does the 'thought experiment' predict the correct answer – although the most indivisible - particle the 'atom' probably arose from such debate. In any event, if such an approach was successful on a regular basis it could be argued that there would be less need for scientific experiment.

Most discussions on TV or radio are chaired by people with scant scientific training. Their background is often in journalism with a university degree in subjects like politics, philosophy, history, education, journalism or performing arts. This does not qualify them to venture into areas of science. Take note; whenever a scientist is talking, the interviewer, instead of interrupting repeatedly as normal, is often conspicuously silent and just thanks the expert for their contribution. Why are there for example, no scientists or medical doctors interviewing people on the main news channels? It gets worse. Politicians and their colleagues are forever citing statistics to cement their view e.g. a 10% reduction in expenses or a 20% increase of funding for some noble cause. Without a denominator these statements are meaningless but hardly ever go challenged because most chairpersons have minimal grasp of even basic statistics or if they ever did, it has been long forgotten. This deficiency prompted chapter 5 on elementary statistics.

This book is not about formal debating techniques that one might witness in university debating societies. It is not designed primarily for academics. It is more involved with informal, impromptu conversations that might arise in a pub, club, changing room, over dinner or at a party. Similar informal debates are popular in radio programmes such as LBC (London Broadcasting Corporation) where members of the public are invited to phone in and voice their opinions.

Good conversation is a dying art and social interaction based solely on discussing controversy may become dull. In one of more his more pensive moments Omid Djalili, the Iranian comedian, suggested there are three levels of conversation: level 1, where people talk about other people; in level 2, they talk about events, and in level 3, they discuss ideas. Although this book is centred mainly around level 3 discussion, it is important to diversify the interchange, if only to maintain interest and attention.

My book has two sections. The first part deals with *Theory and Strategy*, namely debating techniques that might be implemented in defence or attack. The second part is *The Practice* and gives examples of arguments (all fictitious) where these techniques are applied.

Please note that any views expressed are not necessarily those of the author.

PART I

THEORY AND STRATEGY

CHAPTER 1

PRELIMINARY ASSESSMENT

- *Do not bother to argue if there is no chance of winning.* For example, a debate with a Jesuit or Rabbi will rarely be won as they are highly trained, quick-witted, and plausible orators. A gentlemanly draw is the most you should expect. Discussions between opposing cultures/religions e.g. Jewish and Palestinian or the Sunni and Shiite divisions of Islam may become heated. Furthermore, the majority of politicians are professional debaters and will be well rehearsed in most relevant topics. Approach with caution!

- *If the debate is between family and friends, avoid making the argument personal* and especially do not be rude about their partner! For example, if the discussion is about tax avoidance, then it is best to avoid asking 'if you had won £1000 on a gamble would you not tell the tax authorities?' It is better to rephrase in the third person: 'if someone had won a large sum on a lottery should they not inform the tax authorities? In the UK, lottery wins are tax exempt, but this varies from one country to the next.

- *Avoid being judgemental.* In other words, do not describe your opponent as dishonest, devious, etc. If you do, then the debate will become heated. Some interviewers are deliberately judgemental in the full knowledge it will be annoying and that *an angry person is likely to let slip important information* or a particular view that otherwise might be concealed.

Cartoon 1.1

- *If you disagree strongly with a statement, try saying nothing or just make a gentle nod* especially where you wish to maintain a friendly relationship. Failing that, make a bland response like 'I'm not so sure about that' or 'I have heard that is a popular view'.
- Here is a useful potentially calming statement allegedly voiced by an American senator:

  'You're entitled to your own opinion, but you aren't entitled to your own facts.'

- *If you disagree, try to use the third person* e.g. 'others might take a different stance on that'; or 'there are other ways of looking at this'. Avoid saying 'I disagree' etc. Also see Socratic Jujitsu below.

- *Define the terms of argument and individual words.* So many arguments become intense unnecessarily because key words are being used in a different manner. It is basically a semantic issue but if this aspect is not identified early, the conversation may go round in circles and produce exasperation at the very least.

Cartoon 1.2

Here are some words that regularly provoke confused debate:

Englishness or Britishness. Very difficult to define precisely. It is best reserved for light-hearted discussions. In the same vein, use of the term 'The British People' is popular with politicians. It is meaningless but more often indicates 'in my view'.

Freedom. This always needs definition before debate. Many consider freedom to be relative rather than absolute.

Libertarian values. This is a whole philosophy that is not necessarily political, although there are variants of it. It has multiple facets encompassed by the statement: 'a world in which all individuals are sovereign over their own lives and are not forced to sacrifice their values for the benefit of others. We believe that respect for individual rights is the essential precondition for a free and prosperous world, that force and fraud must be banished from human relationships, and that only through freedom can peace and prosperity be realized. Consequently, we defend each person's right to engage in any activity that is peaceful and honest' (from the Libertarian Party).

Life. Agreement on this word is essential prior to any debate about termination of pregnancy. There are various scientific definitions of which a popular one is 'the ability to sustain an independent existence and reproduce'. Most foetuses will die if delivered before 22-24 weeks, thus they are not capable of an independent existence – and even after 24 weeks they are heavily dependent on an incubator, medical support etc. This is the basis of the 24-week guideline in UK law. Some define life as beginning from the moment of fertilisation, others from the earliest time the heartbeat is detectable which is 5-6 weeks using vaginal ultrasound.

Fit (physically). The word 'fit' has multiple meanings even in the medical sense. A person may feel fit but have disease such as tuberculosis, diabetes, early cancer or even AIDS. Someone who can run 100 metres without feeling breathless would likely be very fit and someone would be considered reasonably healthy (although not necessarily athletic) with a BMI (Body Mass Index) of 20-25.

Beauty. This is a highly subjective term with considerable variation according to fashion, religious, racial, gender and age-related issues.

Normal. There is the lay sense of this word (probably impossible to characterize precisely) and the well-defined statistical meaning as explained in the statistics chapter below. It is important to agree which version of the word is being used.

Intelligence. There are multiple definitions. Decades ago, it was defined according to performance on intelligence quotient (IQ) measurement such as the Stanford-Binet test. This proved useful in school selection procedures, but it has been replaced by measures of general ability or cognitive function. Estimates of IQ do not measure all aspects of higher mental ability such as creativity and they are susceptible to cultural influences or prior educational training.

Appropriate or measured. A new law may be under consideration and advocates could argue that it is appropriate and not too restrictive of, e.g. behaviour. The term needs to be defined carefully with examples.

Frequently or common. These words are used regularly in debate, but they rarely defined precisely. For an exact definition one would have to resort to some form of statistics. Thus, you could propose that 'frequently' meant an action (for example tax evasion) undertaken by more than 75% of the population etc. In a similar vein, there are the terms 'majority' and 'minority'. On their own they convey no meaning until defined appropriately e.g. greater than 90% or less than 10%. In attack, you could ask whether 51% meant a majority or whether 49% meant a minority! Rarely do debaters have solid figures available and this can be a source of weakness you may wish to exploit.

Consciousness. There are several definitions. For the practising doctor it usually indicates being awake and responsive. Elsewhere it is the ability to have internal thought and make free decisions. The discussion can become quite emotional. There are some scientific experiments related to this topic e.g. by Benjamin Libet (see debate 14) – so you should be familiar with his work before venturing forth.

Free Will. This is tied in with the consciousness debate as above. Be wary of personal anecdotes. This debate requires a sound knowledge of neuroscience.

a) Buying time to think

Create a Breathing Space. The most successful debaters/interviewers are very quick-witted. They may well have run through a particular argument many times previously. Like a skilled chess-player they may be able o predict your next move. It often helps to know how to create a breathing space to gather your thoughts, so here are some diversionary tactics:

- **Wait for the full mouth.** If the conversation occurs during a meal, watch your opponent's eating habits and pose your question/response when their mouth is full. This gives you time to think of your next comment.

Cartoon 1.3

- **Wait for breathing in.** If your adversary talks a lot, they have to take a breath sooner or later, so wait until they draw breath and then intervene. If this technique (and the one above) is used against *you,* counter it by eating small amounts.

- **Deliberately make your point in a vague manner.** Do this in the hope that your opponent might explain it back to you more clearly and that it will appear then to be *his* idea. Barristers are fond of this technique in court particularly when addressing the judge. Here is an example:

  Prosecuting barrister:
  My lord: if we put together all the available evidence and exclude what is agreed and not agreed then it is clear that the defence argument just rests on two flimsy points that we have already rebutted. Is it not simply a case therefore of *res ipsa loquitor* (the facts speak for themselves) and that there is no case to answer?

  Judge: So you are basically saying that you reject the defence argument?

  Prosecuting barrister: So well put, My lord.

- **Mutter or mumble, covering up your mouth so you appear to have responded.** This could be used as a defence strategy if you are not sure what to say. You will be asked to repeat yourself, but you will have secured a short breathing space to compose a reply.

- **Create a diversion.** Over a meal, if you are losing the debate and need time to think, create a diversion. For example: knock over a wine glass or drop food / cutlery on floor. Offer to go to the kitchen to clear up. Feign stomach pain and go to the toilet. Similarly:

- **Throw a dead cat on the table.** This is a favourite ploy of lawyers and politicians. It is a trick to be used if you are losing badly and need a major breathing space. It does not really matter what the debate is about, just say something completely outrageous, true or false *to force a change of subject.*

o   When it was clear at a conference interview during 2015 that Donald Trump was not faring well in the election campaign, he said 'I'm going to ban all Muslims from entering the country'. That shocked everyone and it immediately turned the debate topic onto immigration and away from his then poor campaign performance.

o   Several years ago, I was in Court as a rather inexperienced expert witness for the claimant. Allegedly, she had fallen over backwards on a slippery floor at work, sustaining a nasty blow to the back of her head. There were multiple complaints, and she was unable to work. It all seemed quite plausible to me. The defending barrister asked me one simple question – a 'dead cat' - 'what if the accident never happened?' I was thrown completely by this and the judge had to explain the question to me! The barrister then said mockingly 'shall we start over again then?' - repeating the original question. Total humiliation: but he was implying that the defendant was a complete charlatan who was basically inventing everything for financial gain. The subsequent discussion was then focussed entirely on whether the plaintiff was telling the truth and not about her alleged disability, much to the annoyance of the prosecuting barrister.

Cartoon 1.4

b)   Delaying techniques.

If you are stuck for an answer, there are several dodges to give you time for thought and yet appear in control:

•   *That's a very interesting/great question. Or say 'thank-you for giving me the opportunity to address these difficult issues'* and then talk off the point. You will be lucky to get away without answering the question in a formal interview.

•   *Criticise the topic itself.* If the questioner asks about alleged injustice, say something like 'it depends on what you mean by 'unjust' or proclaim loudly 'that's not the question!'

•   *Repeat your opponents' question* or statement as if to imply they had not spoken clearly or that you may have not understood their statement e.g. 'are you asking me why I went to the Green Peace rally?' Or: 'are you asking me whether I believe in global warming?' This gives you time to compose a response. It often pays to *act as if you are confused by the question* thus you can gain thinking time by asking for further clarification. For example: *'I'm not sure I completely understand your question'*

• Say *'before I answer that may I just say this...'.* You may be able to escape a difficult point. Politicians implement this manoeuvre all the time. For example, if the conversation concerns illness or an accident affecting a famous person, you might respond first by expressing condolences for the affected person and/or their family. An experienced interviewer will simply re-iterate or re-phrase the original question, but you will have given yourself some thinking time!

• *Answer the question with a question.* If your opponent uses a word such as 'moderate' 'measured' 'elitist' or 'appropriate' then ask what he actually means by these adjectives. This can be unsettling for your adversary as well as giving you time to compose your reply.

• *Accept multiple questions, then answer just the ones you like.* Tony Blair, the former British Prime Minister used this approach extensively and skilfully. Note: the experienced interviewer asks just one short, sharp question.

• *Ignore the question completely and talk about another issue you consider important.*

• *Answer the question but make the same point in multiple ways.* You can play for time this way, by reinforcing your point with examples and metaphors. Politicians are proficient at this. It fills up interview time and might leave less opportunity for more difficult questions later.

• *State what you are not going to talk about.* This is a devious trick, popular with experienced debaters who wish to buy time and attack someone of opposing beliefs, while criticising them indirectly and then deflecting the conversation onto a topic of their choice (see Cartoon 1.5)

Cartoon 1.5

- **Exploit an interruption.** Conversely, you might be able to turn an interruption to your advantage. Thus, if there is a break in the questions and you cannot remember where you left off, ask your opponent 'where were we?' Your opponent may need to pause for thought or have forgotten also but either way it gives you time to generate a good response.

In the same context:

- *Ask yourself a question!* Again, a regular device of some politicians. Having given a superficial response to the issue, they might say 'do I believe there should be a further cash injection into the social housing budget? No'. 'Do I believe that interest rates should be lowered in the current fiscal year? Yes'. In this way a member of parliament (MP) can take control of an interview completely as in the next point:

- *Take control of an interview or debate.* A useful technique is to end your response with a sentence that prompts a question you wish to answer. The debate could proceed as follows:

MP: *There has certainly been an increase in the number of nurses now working in the NHS compared to the detailed analysis published 5 years ago.*

Hopefully, this will promote a further question:

Interviewer: *Well, what were the figures 5 years back?*

MP: *they can be divided into changes in district nurses and hospital-based nurses etc*

Interviewer: *Please tell us more*

And so on.

- Be cautious using the phrase *'the science says or tells us this'.* Generally, scientific evidence is far more reliable than peoples' opinions or quotations from newspapers, social media etc. 'Follow the science' was a popular phrase. If your opponent is scientifically trained (a 'technocrat'), he may well counter that scientists do not agree on a particular issue. This aspect was particularly relevant when government scientific advisers were trying to formulate a policy on how to manage Covid-19 infection. The Prime Minister at the time (Boris Johnson) stated that the science advised for example: use of a face mask, avoiding social contact, staying indoors, washing hands frequently etc. However, the scientific advisers were not unanimous in their recommendations. Some regarded use of disposable face masks by the public to be futile unless they were of the particularly sophisticated (and expensive) variety e.g. FFP3.

CHAPTER 2

BASIC TECHNIQUES IN DEBATE

Disarm your opponent by appearing to agree. Try saying: 'I think you are absolutely right on that'. This is fine if it is sincere but often it's a trap, so beware if it is applied against you. It has been termed 'Socratic Jujitsu' by author Jennifer Hancock (2017). It is a very popular strategy with civil servants. Look out for their next point that may include statements with which you do *not* agree.

Cartoon 2.1

How to say 'yes' or 'no' without using that word directly. Here are some phrases exploited mercilessly by Civil Servants: for 'No':

- Well, yes and no
- I think that might be difficult to achieve
- Let's see what Sir Henley-Jones thinks about this
- Why don't we have another meeting to discuss this in greater depth?
- I think this a very important issue that clearly merits a full enquiry

Here are some ways of saying 'yes' in a non-committal fashion:

- It is certainly worth putting on the table and looking at
- That is obviously something that should be addressed in future
- You definitely have a good point there.
- I couldn't agree more in a way but let's see what happens
- We are working very hard to secure what you suggest

Cartoon 2.2

Alternatively, you can go to one extreme as shown in this example taken from the book and subsequent TV series 'Yes Minister' where the Minister (James Hackett) questions his cabinet secretary (Sir Humphrey):

James Hackett: *Are you going to support my view that the Civil Service is over-manned and feather-bedded, or not? Yes or no? Straight answer.*

Sir Humphrey: *Well Minister, if you ask me for a straight answer, then I shall say that, as far as we can see, looking at it by and large, taking one thing with another in terms of the average of departments, then in the final analysis it is probably true to say, that at the end of the day, in general terms, you would probably find that, not to put too fine a point on it, there probably wasn't very much in it one way or the other. As far as one can see, at this stage.*

Conversely if you are feeling aggressive and really want an answer, try this type of question:

- Are you going to authorise this, *yes or no*? The danger is an even more evasive response.

Ways of appearing to apologise. Thus, the words 'sorry' or 'apologise' are used but only indirectly. Be wary of an apparent apology that is followed by the word 'but':

- I am so sorry to hear of your problems with our human resources department but...
- We are absolutely committed to offering the highest possible service and I apologise that we have not got back to you sooner to deal with your concerns.
- Thank you for giving us the opportunity to address your concerns with our office (yuk!)

Attack the 'They' word. So many people use a sentence such as:

- They say that the cost of housing is due to rise next month.
- According to what they say, income tax will rise sharply in the next budget.

Most often this is something read or heard on social media, newspapers or in casual conversation. This is your time to pounce and ask, 'who are 'they'. What is the evidence?' Rarely will it be forthcoming. Keep asking for evidence, evidence, evidence. Of course, it helps if you have some evidence of your own!

Referral to Research. A popular phrase is 'research suggests that'. Usually this means that the user has heard something on TV or social media. Once more you should ask for evidence of the alleged research. Who wrote the article? Did it come from a respected peer-reviewed scientific journal?

Lean forward to convey honesty and commitment. Lean backward to convey omniscience. Focus on your opponent's eyes.

Cartoon 2.3

Use emotion. As long as this comes across as sincere it may help swing the balance. Sincerity from a politician often arouses suspicion. Phrases like 'to be quite honest with you' or 'to be totally frank' should be regarded as warning signals! Feigned or real tears usually signals the end of a debate. Laughter or sniggering will annoy your opponent. Use with caution.

Use hyperbole. That is, exaggerate to reinforce your point. For example:

'All Labour party members are hell-bent on taking over the nation's wealth for themselves'.

'It is absolutely clear that all those people on social benefits are scroungers who have never done a decent day's work in their lives'.

Damning with feigned (or faint) praise.

Here are a few quotes:

- o 'Democracy is a device that ensures we shall be governed no better than we deserve.' (George Bernard Shaw)

- o 'Mr Attlee (former British Prime Minister) is a very modest man. Indeed, he has a lot to be modest about.' (Winston Churchill)

- o 'That's a bit of a curate's egg is it not?' The curate's egg was mostly unfit to eat but out of politeness it is described as not all that bad.

- o If someone (usually a politician) has been fired say, for misconduct in office it is often said when explaining why he left office: 'No, not at all, he just wanted to spend more time with his family.'

Use multiple negatives in your question or response. Many find this confusing and indeed it is difficult sometimes to keep a cool head in this context. To resolve the question, ask for it to be repeated and divide the number of negatives by two. If there is no remainder, then it should be a positive statement. If there is a remainder, then it is negative. Unfortunately, it is not always that simple as there may be difficulty in deciding what is a negative. Here are examples:

- 'It is not true that there is no more money available for our project'. Two negatives equal a positive so there is money available.

- 'Many newspapers are not selling well, so there has never been a more important time not to subscribe to one'. Two negatives equal a positive, so you should take out a newspaper subscription.

- 'Were it not for the speedy actions of my colleague we would not be in such a favourable position as we are now'. Our position is favourable. Once more, two negatives equal a positive

- 'There is simply not enough time not to take this decision (positive!) because if we don't, then nothing will happen (another positive)'. We must decide at once, otherwise there will be no change. Two negatives followed by another two!

Cartoon 2.4

- He was very good at not doing what he didn't want to do. Two negatives, so he was able to avoid doing undesirable things.
- A cabinet minister said: 'I don't think the public are going to buy the idea that by raising National Insurance, we are not breaching our manifesto pledge not to breach taxes. That's simply semantics'. This was a quote from The Sunday Times July 25th 2021. See if you can understand it! The public will realise there is a breach of the manifesto pledge.

Cartoons 2.5

Employ complex sentences. For example:

- What was God about to do that he had to send his only son to Earth to stop him (i.e. God) from doing it?'
- What was the European Union about to do that we had to have a referendum to stop them doing it?
- Here is one from 'Yes Prime Minister'
  ..."Thinking back on what I said and what you said and what I said you said, or what they may say I said you said, or what they may have thought I said I thought you thought, or they may say I said, I thought you said I thought...'
- It's not the question that we should lie back and do nothing. We simply have no option.

Try to detect Lying. Lying provokes activity in a nucleus in the temporal lobes known as the amygdala. This results in facial flushing, sweating, changes in heart rate and blood pressure. Skin resistance decreases because of sweating and this change can be measured by the 'psychogalvanic reflex'. Unfortunately, with repeated untruths many of the traditional signs of lying disappear – a form of deconditioning. There is lack of consensus on how best to detect a liar but here are some of the main contenders that might allow you to detect a fabrication:

- Increased facial sweating or flushing
- Covering up the mouth
- Double blink sign. The liar blinks infrequently and then there is a double blink or several blinks in quick succession
- The liar looks down and usually to the right.
- Touching or rubbing the nose, eyes, ear, or neck.
- Pulling away the collar from the neck.
- Fingers in the mouth
- Generally fidgety, hair grooming
- Tendency to avoid answering question directly
- Palms are concealed – usually in pockets or behind the back
- Excess use of stalling words, such as 'mmm'; 'er'; 'you know'.

Metaphors, similes, analogies and proverbs. There is considerable overlap between these four figures of speech and their differences when it comes to debate is not too important. Knowledge of a few might suggest intellectual superiority. They are extremely popular with politicians presumably because, if necessary, *they can be re-interpreted later.*

Metaphors. These are figures of speech that state a comparison directly such as:

- Love is a game of war. Thus, in love there are few rules, it's like a battle
- Parliament is a nest of worms. This implies that politicians are untrustworthy, continually changing their view.
- His face was thunder. A look of extreme anger.
- A black swan. An unexpected event.
- Carpetbagger or parachute candidate. A non-local candidate who is brought in to help swing the vote.
- Sacrificial lamb. In politics it is used to describe a candidate who has no chance of election.
- Pork barrel. Use of government funds to secure votes
- Mud raking. Looking for any incriminating information
- To re-invent the wheel. To waste time by duplicating something that has already been invented
- The elephant in the room. The glaringly obvious problem
- Glass ceiling. An invisible barrier. Usually applied to women and minorities who are denied promotion
- Cut the Gordian knot. To solve an impossible problem at a stroke. This goes back to Greek mythology concerning a peasant, Gordius who tied a knot that no-one could disentangle until Alexander the Great sliced through it with on stroke of his sword

Similes are comparable but usually contain the words 'like' or 'as' to make a comparison. For example:

- She was cunning as a fox.
- He is slippery as mercury.
- He is strong as an ox
- Slow, like watching paint dry.

Analogies are like similes but contain an explanatory phrase:

- that's like rearranging deck chairs on the Titanic'. Unnecessary attention to detail in a crisis.

- That's like papering over the cracks on a wall. Just covering up a mess.
- A double-edged sword. Something that might result in either benefit or harm.

Cartoon 2.6

Proverbs are popular sayings to exemplify a truth or piece of advice. Here are a few:

- We'll just end up just kicking the can down the road again. A delaying tactic.
- That is like gilding a lily. Trying to improve something that is already perfect.
- It is like having one foot on the accelerator and the other on the brake. Unsure whether to proceed or hold back.
- Fear is a beast that feeds on attention. Fear worsens with increasing focus.
- A problem shared is a problem halved.

- Poisoned chalice. A tempting opportunity that could easily go wrong. It is like the Trojan Horse ploy used in Greek mythology. This apparent friendly gift contained a small group of elite soldiers. Thus, you could say 'that's a bit of a Trojan Horse'.
- People in glass houses should not throw stones. Do not criticise others when you are vulnerable to criticism yourself.
- Crossing the Rubicon. The Rubicon is a river that Julius Caesar crossed in 49 BC thus precipitating civil war. It applies to making a decision from which there is no turning back.
- Necessity is the mother of invention. Discoveries are made at times of greater need e.g. wartime.
- Got him over a barrel. Someone in a very weak position.
- We are caught between Scylla and Charybdis. In Greek mythology, sailors were confronted by Scylla (a six-headed sea-monster) and Charybdis (a deadly whirlpool). Thus, it is impossible to know what to do. Also 'between a rock and a hard place' or 'between the devil and the deep blue sea'.
- Cut the mustard. Come up to expectation.
- Sword of Damocles. Damocles was placed in a position of great responsibility, but a sword was hanging over him. It refers to a perilous situation with an unpredictable outcome.
- Pass muster. To reach an acceptable standard.
- What goes around comes around. If you do something unpleasant the consequences may ultimately affect you.
- Cut to the chase. Get to the point.
- Horses for courses. Everyone has different skills for a particular task. You have to choose the most suitable person.
- Square the circle. Trying to do the impossible
- Post hoc ergo proctor hoc. After the fact, therefore because of it. Regularly shortened to post hoc. It is often mis-used to infer causality where one event follows another. Similarly: 'association does not mean causation'.
- Ex Cathedra statement. Literally means 'from the chair'. Originally it referred to statements by Popes who are assumed to be

infallible. The term is regularly applied to pompous statements made by famous people, not necessarily supported by facts.

- When you decide you divide.
- If you throw mud, it sticks. If you make an accusation (whether true or false) it is hard to get rid of it
- The only thing necessary for the triumph of evil is that good men do nothing (Edmund Burke)

Special pleading. This refers to the ploy that normal rules of logic cannot or should not be applied in a particular case. The tactic is used sometimes by psychic healers, clairvoyants, homeopathic therapists, Jehovah's Witnesses, and other deeply religious people. It is implied that faith transcends logic and science. Winning an argument in this context is difficult unless you have scientific evidence, which is rarely present. There are scientific trials, published in reputable journals like The Lancet that concern homeopathic medicines most of which show zero benefit. Some argue that faith plus placebo is as powerful as formal medical therapy.

Lack of evidence against the effectiveness of a new medicine / therapy means it could still work.

This strategy is used often to shift the onus of proof to whoever doubts an association or proposal. Thus, if a new form of treatment for say painful joints is introduced and some find it useful but there are no completed scientific trials it could be argued that you cannot prove the new therapy does *not* work. Hence the saying:

'Absence of evidence is not evidence of absence'.

You could reply by saying that the onus of proof lies with the user of the new measure.

Beware a world expert talking about areas outside his realm of expertise.

A Nobel Laureate or other person held in high esteem may make a statement outside their field of expertise. Often this results in uncritical acceptance of their declaration. Just because a person has made important scientific discoveries in one field does not mean they will be right in all domains of knowledge. Kary Mullis, the Nobel prize-winner awarded for his discovery of the polymerase chain reaction (used for detecting minute amounts of bacteria or viruses) asserted incorrectly that HIV (the virus) did not lead to AIDS (the disease). Linus Pauling (winner of Nobel prizes for chemistry and peace) claimed that vitamin C helped prevent or cure the common cold and cancer; neither statement has been verified scientifically. Arthur Conan Doyle, the medical doctor and author of the famous Sherlock Holmes novels appeared to believe in the existence of fairies. This overall concept is expanded in David Robson's book 'The Intelligence Trap' (2019).

FALLACIES

- **The Bandwagon Fallacy.** This suggests that because an idea is very popular then it must be correct. For example, homeopathy is popular therefore it must be a valid form of treatment. It is a form of circular reasoning. Also see the section below on 'Myside Bias'.
- **The Panglossian fallacy.** In Voltaire's satirical novel 'Candide' (1759), Dr Pangloss was a fictional 'Professor of metaphysico-cosmo-nigology'. He believed that we lived in the best of all possible worlds and that there were logical explanations for pain and turmoil. No-one suffered without good reason.

When opposing change, some people state:

o   We always did things this way, so what's the point of changing?
o   People always believed that to be the case so we should just accept it
o   We are where we are
o   That's just how it is.

In medicine, some will argue that an observed outcome is the necessary outcome.

Allied to this is the belief that low-income countries like parts of Africa are destined to remain thus and will never progress to a high-income economy like the West. This concept is incorrect as elucidated in the book: 'Factfulness' by Hans Rosling (2018)

- **Guilty by association**. Here, someone links an opponent to a demonised group or untrustworthy person. Thus, the opponent's view cannot be right because of his 'wrong' connections'.

  'I wouldn't trust a word that chap says. He supports the QAnon movement, doesn't he?'

- **Straw Man tactic**. This is based on the principle that it is easier to knock over a straw man than a real person. It is an intentional *change of subject* or *misrepresentation* of an argument, often introduced because the new topic may be easier to defend (or attack).

If someone states that pollution by humans causes global warming, then the Straw Man response might be:

'So what you are saying is that floods, hurricanes, slow-running clocks, melting ice-creams are all our fault?

This is not exactly what was proposed but it could result in a change of subject. Beware of someone who responds with the phrase 'so what you are saying is... ' or 'in other words you believe that...'

In 1952, President Nixon was accused of trousering $18,000 of campaign funds. In his response he talked instead about a dog (Checkers) that had been donated to his daughter, how much she adored it and that he intended to keep it. This is a sort-of straw man evasion - although it overlaps with throwing a dead cat on the table (see above).

Cartoon 2.7

- **The Steel Man tactic.** This is the opposite of the Straw Man manoeuvre and popular with governments. Prior a debate that you may wish to oppose, your group engages in role play i.e. to adopt the mind-set of the opposition. Thus, in preparation for your own argument you construct the strongest version of your opponent's position, to ensure your counter-arguments are more convincing. In less formal situations you may attempt to re-express the other person's position so clearly that they might respond: 'Thanks, I wish I'd thought of putting it that way'.

- **The Nuremberg Defence.** This is an attempt to avoid responsibility when the person concerned was 'just following superior orders'. It goes back to the trials of crimes by former Nazi leaders after World War II. According to International Law this is not a permissible defence. Outside wartime scenarios a similar plea may be used by civilians when defending actions in organised crime, illegal management of money etc.

- **False dichotomy.** Many debates revolve about something that is either right or wrong, true or false, guilty or not guilty, Capitalist or Marxist etc. It is important to identify such binary strategy in your opponent and counter them by pointing out, for example, that there is more often a *continuum of values* between two extremes. Such polarisation is popular with dictators and tyrants alike. Here are some examples:

Apart from a small minority, all political demonstrations are the same. Just a load of thugs wanting a good fight with the police and the opportunity to loot a few stores for luxury goods.

There are just two types of cyclists: the ones that drive all over the road getting in your way at junctions, and others who ride right in front of your car with just a few that stick to the cycle lanes.

You would need to point out that the examples cited are extreme scenarios that are not representative of the bigger picture. You could use the 'aggregate' point i.e. that most demonstrations or most cyclists are well behaved and that there may be *selective recall bias* (see below) favouring exceptions.

- **Attack the player not the ball.** Sometimes known as the *Ad Hominem* (against the man) fallacy. Thus, if you do not like an idea (the ball), attack the person who proposes the concept. Dig into their political past, whether there are any conflicts of interest in a new project (particularly financial); whether a family member has a vested influence. See debate number 4. Inevitably the debate will become heated. This approach was common when discussing Boris Johnson, prior to his appointment as British Prime Minister. Those who disagreed with his proposals, sometimes brought up aspects of his past (multiple affairs, divorce, illegitimate children) which will serve as a distraction, although they may have nothing to do with the issue under consideration. It could be viewed as a variant of the Straw Man tactic.

Cartoon 2.8

- **Slippery slope tactic.** If you do not like a concept, you could suggest this might be the start of worse things to come. For example, if it were proposed to de-criminalise soft recreational drugs such as cannabis then it could be argued that this would be the top of a slippery slope, on course for legalisation of hard drugs like cocaine, lysergic acid, amphetamine etc.
- **Over-generalisation fallacy.** This implies that if one person in a social group misbehaves then all its members must be bad. This is similar to the false dichotomy fallacy cited above i.e. if one cyclist acts badly on the road then all must be equally bad
- **Red Herrings.** This refers to the use of irrelevant information to distract your opponent from the main topic of debate.

It may be argued that passive smoking is dangerous but because people will always over-eat and drink too much alcohol, then there will be no beneficial effect even if smoking is banned.

The crime rate in London has increased recently, however the weather has worsened as well, so who knows if crime has really gone up? It could be connected to the awful weather conditions. The counter to this could be 'association is not evidence of causation'. See below.

Cartoon 2.9

- **Circular reasoning.** This is similar to 'begging the question'. The debater begins with what they are trying to conclude. Just because the premises may be true does not necessarily mean the conclusions are correct.

  - *The Bible is the Word of God because God tells us it is - in the Bible.*

  - *Anthony always votes wisely because everyone knows he votes for the Conservative party*

  - *Occupants of the Guantanamo Bay prison in Cuba are terrorists. They have not been subject to a fair trial but there is no need to – they are all terrorists*

  - *Free speech being a privilege rather than a right, it is proper for a society to suspend free speech when it feels threatened.*

Here is an example of circular reasoning from Alice's adventures in Wonderland (Lewis Carroll)

But I don't want to go among mad people," Alice remarked.

"Oh, you can't help that," said the Cat: "we're all mad here. I'm mad. You're mad."

"How do you know I'm mad?" said Alice.

"You must be," said the Cat, "or you wouldn't have come here."

Note that the examples above are also *non sequiturs* i.e., illogical statements.

- **The appeal to fear fallacy**. Here someone tries to create support for their idea or product by attempting to show the dangers of an alternative. It is used unethically in marketing to promote sales by suggesting that a competitor's product is worthless and possibly harmful.

CHAPTER 3

MORE STRATEGIES

What to do if you do not understand or forget the meaning of a word or phrase. Instead of asking for an explanation – (which would declare your ignorance and inferiority) ask e.g., 'what do you actually mean by hegemony' – or whatever word you do not comprehend. It almost implies that the other person does not fully understand the word they have just used!

Cartoon 3.1

"If people are upset because you've forgotten something, console them by letting them know you didn't forget—you just weren't remembering." (From Winnie the Pooh by AA Milne)

Listen for signs of a feeble response by your opponent. For example, the use of phrases like:

- Surely it is true that - or just the word 'surely'
- It is my understanding that
- It is generally agreed that
- Everyone knows that
- In my experience
- Most people would agree that
- The British people know this is the correct course of action. A pompous phrase favoured by politicians. The 'British People' are impossible to define. It usually means 'what I believe'

This is your signal to attack!

Slightly more subtle but just as weak, is the use of phrases such as 'You *would not expect* this to happen'.

For example:

- If the price of houses went up, then *you would expect* mortgages to become more difficult to obtain. This is probably true, but there needs to be evidence, not speculation
- If people spent more time reading and less time watching TV, *you would expect* them to be better educated and less obese. A plausible statement but again there needs to be proper evidence

Never admit ignorance. If you do, you will be vulnerable. Nod your head wisely, say 'yes' quietly and respond with phrases like:

- 'That may be the case but...' or 'I have heard it said'. Then try to change the subject as quickly as possible!
- If someone asks if you have read a book or article (and you have not) never admit it. Say something like: 'yes, I did read some of it' even if it was just the introduction!
- If you are discussing something specialised in say, politics or science, say 'it's quite difficult keeping up with current research on this topic, but my understanding is that....'

In a similar manner, doctors are just as guilty. If an obscure disease is not understood they use fancy terms like 'idiopathic'; 'autochthonous' 'essential'; 'abiotrophy'; 'primary' or 'essential'. One of the latest is 'neurodegeneration'. It sounds amazing but is nothing more than a cover-up for our lack of understanding of the relentless progression and death of nerve cells found in conditions like Parkinson's disease or Alzheimer's disease.

Try to pigeon-hole opponent. That is, label him/her as a lefty, communist, fascist, aristocrat etc. This is a judgemental approach that will annoy your adversary, as it will imply that their responses are ill-considered dogma. The inevitable response is to deny your assessment. Conversely, *avoid revealing your own political/religious beliefs* as your opponent might try to stereotype <u>you</u> and make numerous assumptions about your personal opinions which may not necessarily be true.

Avoid the Blame Game. It is human nature to blame someone for events that go wrong. How could they be blameless?

- In Russia, syphilis was called the Polish disease. In Poland it was called the German disease. In Germany it was called the French disease.

- o The pandemic influenza of 1918 was called the Spanish 'flu
- o Covid-19 was sometimes called Chinese flu.

The natural temptation to blame someone or something should be resisted because it is usually counter-productive and may lead to cessation of rational thought

Quote sayings from famous people. It is a good plan to have a few quotes up your sleeve. It conveys erudition i.e., wisdom. Popular sources are Winston Churchill, Voltaire, Schopenhauer, Oscar Wilde. Here are a few examples:

- Democracy is the worst form of government except for all the others - Winston Churchill (British prime minister)
- A statue has never been set up in honour of a critic - Jean Sibelius (Finnish composer)
- All truth passes through three stages: first, it is ridiculed; second, it is violently opposed;
  third, it is accepted as self-evident - Arthur Schopenhauer (German philosopher)
- The cynic is a man who knows the price of everything and the value of nothing - Oscar Wilde (English playwright)
- All the world's a stage, and all the men and women merely players. (William Shakespeare, As You Like It)
- If you can look into the seeds of time and say which grain will grow and which will not, speak then to me. William Shakespeare, Macbeth
- Progress was always due to unreasonable people because reasonable people wanted to use the system as it was, not change it - George Bernard Shaw (British playwright). You might counter this by saying 'if it's not broken don't fix it'
- A bureaucracy comes about when a body of people who have come together for a purpose, change that purpose to the

perpetuation of the body - Edward de Bono (English philosopher and inventor of lateral thinking)

- An investment in knowledge pays the best interest - Benjamin Franklin (Founding father of USA)
- The more I practice the luckier I get - Tiger Woods (American golfer)
- Hell hath no fury like a woman scorned - William Congreve (English playwright and poet)
- Doctors are men who prescribe medicines of which they know little, to cure diseases of which they know less, in human beings of whom they know nothing - Voltaire (French writer historian and philosopher). His real name was Francois-Marie Arouet
- There are three kinds of lies: lies, damned lies and statistics. A statement attributed to Benjamin Disraeli (British prime minister) and Mark Twain (American writer; real name Samuel Langhorne Clemens).

Cartoon 3.2

Make a joke or recite some humorous sayings. If the debate is getting heated this is a good way of defusing the quarrel. Try to memorise a few jokes that could be brought into the conversation. Here are some examples:

- 'If God had intended politicians to think he would have given them brains.'
- 'I don't know the answer to your question, nor do I know anyone who would know nor someone they would know who would know…'
- 'If all Victorian medicines were thrown into the sea, only the fish would suffer.' (Sir Derrick Dunlop, founder of the UK Committee on Safety of Medicine)
- 'The art of medicine consists of *amusing* the *patient while nature* cures the disease.' (Voltaire)
- Pompous doctors, when talking about a rare condition sometimes say 'in my experience, this is how the disease presents'. Others may emphasize further: 'in my case series' and finally. 'time and time again I have seen this happen…'
- 'Behind every great fortune lies a great crime.' (Balzac)

Attack the detail of an idea. If someone comes up with a new concept that you do not like, instead of attacking the general proposal, attack the detail. It may distract your opponent.

- If the notion is to establish a monorail system for central London, you might respond by saying that the Unions would oppose it, it would be noisy and very expensive to build and operate and it would obstruct light for nearby buildings.
- Identity cards. These have been proposed many times in the UK without success. Possible responses include: 'it would be impossible to have them printed in time'. 'People would be able to forge them immediately and sell them on the black market'. 'It's tantamount to a police state'
- Free University entrance for everyone. The idea is to allow everyone who wishes to attend University for the first year, followed by an examination to determine who may continue. The counter response for those who do not like the proposal

might be 'this would be completely unaffordable and where would we put all those students' etc.

Cartoon 3.3

Pretend not to have properly understood a statement or new idea. Pretend to be confused. For example:

'Do you mean this literally or metaphorically?'
'What do you mean by *now* – today, tomorrow or next week?'
'Is your suggestion a hope, aspiration or statement of real intent?'
'Do you really think that the British people will approve of this?

Start by praising the subject and then attacking it ('Socratic jujitsu'):

'I think you have an excellent idea in theory and I totally agree with much of the concept but on this occasion I cannot see how it would possibly work in practice..'

Similarly:

Look out for a subtle change of subject. This is analogous to the Straw Man tactic.

If you say, 'it's scandalous that Lord Cadogan owns 93 acres of central London (Kensington and Chelsea)'. Your opponent may deflect this point without admitting it is right or wrong and say, 'well what would you do about it?' If you are not focussed, you might comment on the need for action rather than concentrate on the initial accusation of inequality. Try to keep the argument on the main subject and then later, only if required, debate the methods of rectifying the problem.

In general, understating your case is a more powerful approach than overstating it.

In World War II Hitler constantly bragged about the number of British planes shot down to which Churchill replied, *'If Herr Hitler does not cease these misrepresentations, his reputation for veracity may be impugned'.* A mixture of understatement and sarcasm. Overstated remarks are easily identified and quickly rebutted by your adversary.

Cartoon 3.4

Ask leading questions.

Friendly enquiries are simple without any expectation or desire for a particular answer. Leading questions are strategies to encourage the respondent to agree with the questioner and possibly incriminate themselves. They are popular with trial lawyers who hope that such questions to a defendant, for example, might cause them to admit their guilt. Interviewers on News programmes use leading questions *ad nauseam* – especially with politicians – but the experienced MP is familiar with this approach and most other ploys to catch them out!

Here are some examples:

- You were in Hornchurch High St on the night of the murder, were you not?
- Isn't it true that you have anti-Semitic views?
- When are you going to sort out this mess you have created?
- Why do you keep contradicting yourself?
- When are you going to stop beating your wife?

An allegedly true, humorous dialogue from Court:

> During cross examination, the prosecuting barrister said, 'After you put arsenic in the soup and served it to your husband, you must have felt remorse for what you were doing?'
>
> 'I did,' she replied.
>
> 'And when was that?'
>
> 'When he asked for more!'

Anecdotes. These can be a double-edged sword. Examples from one's personal life are useful to reinforce your point, but you become vulnerable to attack. If you are debating the police 'stop and search' facility you could say:

'A Jamaican friend of mine was just on his way to his local pub when, for no reason, he was stopped and searched by the police. I think the police are racially prejudiced.'

This anecdote may help reinforce the proposal that police are racially biased but if your opponent has good statistics that proves the contrary, you may lose the debate.

You could counter anecdotes by using the word 'aggregate' with the hope your opponent does not understand it. In essence, the aggregate is short for majority – usually people. This point is expanded in the Statistics section below.

Many interviewers and their respondents like to quote examples from their personal life but in general, *anecdotes are weak debating tactics*. So often debates are simply an exchange of anecdotes. Useful counter responses are:

- One swallow does not make a summer
- That's just an exception that makes the rule
- One-off examples from your personal life prove nothing. We should look at the bigger picture.
- If you look at the aggregate – which is the correct approach – then that would not support your few accounts that have purely anecdotal significance.

The best response of all is based on solid statistical facts.

If you make a mistake in debate, it's probably best to admit it right away. Although this conveys the impression of honesty and might gain support, seasoned debaters and politicians rarely confess to a mistake and try to minimise its importance thereafter.

Compare Like with Like. In July 2014, an Israeli warship fired a shell at a derelict shed on the beach in Gaza City killing four Palestinian children who were playing nearby. When the London Israeli ambassador was questioned about this on TV, he said that the British were just as guilty, having killed several children attending school in bomb raids on Germany in World War II. Firstly, two acts of wrongdoing do not justify either (quote the saying *two wrongs do not make a right*) and secondly this is not a *like with like comparison*. That is, Israeli soldiers would have used modern weapons that were far more accurate than the bombs employed in World War II.

This principle is expanded in more detail in the statistics section (Chapter 5).

Beware of taking the moral high ground. In other words, be cautious about making criticism/being judgemental of your opponent or others whose principles or behaviour you may not like or agree with. For example, you might state that your adversaries' standard of driving is poor and that he ignores speed limits on a regular basis. Your opponent might respond 'you can't talk, did you not get a hefty parking fine quite recently? You could reply that this is not a fair, like with like, comparison and there was no danger to life. However, two wrongs do not make a right. Each item of alleged bad behaviour should be considered on its own, irrespective of other peoples' behaviour

Rhetorical question. This is where you ask a question to which *you know the answer*. If you are talking about knife crime in London, you might ask:

- Perhaps you could remind me how many such crimes were committed last year?
- How many policemen were taken off the streets in the last 5 years?

This is a seemingly innocent tactic that can work well if you know the answer - which you must. It has the capacity to humiliate your opponent.

- 'When did you stop hitting your children?'

This is both a leading question and likely rhetorical if the barrister knows the answer, which he probably does. Whether the answer is to admit or deny the accusation, the issue of beating your children is implied to be correct but the respondent may not have hit his children at all.

Cartoon 3.5

Aggressive strategies

- **Throw mud**
  This is a devious method of attack. If you disagree strongly with your opponents, accuse them of dishonesty, hypocrisy, lying etc.

You can leave it at that, or at some time later, apologise profusely. You have maligned your opponent, possibly falsely but as the saying goes, 'mud sticks'. It will be much harder to get rid of an incorrect accusation than to make one.

- **Interrupt as much as possible.**
  This often distracts your opponents' train of thought. Raise your voice and repeat your point in slightly different ways. In 1997, Jeremy Paxman, the British BBC TV interviewer asked Michael Howard (then Home Secretary) the same question in different forms about dismissal of a prison chief *twelve times!* Interruptions and repetitions of the original question anger your adversaries and make them liable to make statements that may be regretted subsequently. Interviewers use this technique constantly (and successfully) especially against lay people and inexperienced politicians.

If someone produces figures that you do not like, fire back and question their authenticity

This is the practice of questioning the question as discussed in Chapter 1. The technique was used by Donald Trump in the 1980s (and many other occasions) when challenged on TV by Ruth Messinger (New York City Councillor) about the need for and the size of his tax deduction (about $160 million) to support construction of Trump Tower. She said it was a form of corporate welfare allowance! His response was to question the accuracy of this amount, accusing her of making up the figures or just quoting them from the New York Times. He did not admit anything and interrupted continually. Trump then accused the Council of not making subways safe – a form of Straw Man defence to deliberately provoke a change of subject.

The *counter-attack* (which was not used on this occasion) could have been to ask Mr Trump what was the true amount of tax abatement. However, it is rarely that simple!

Use ridicule

This can be an effective weapon, but risks alienating your opponent or an audience depending on their sympathies. No-one likes to hear an audience roar with laughter at your views; it's humiliating. Here is an example taken from William A Rusher's book 'How to Win Arguments' (1981). The debate concerned capital punishment. The point was made that if a proven murderer is given just life imprisonment, he can continue to commit murder without fear of death while in jail. One such prisoner, who became known as the 'Bird Man of Alcatraz,' was an expert on canaries and wrote a book on it. He killed another prison inmate, thus raising the question of what further punishment would he then deserve. In debate, Rusher says to his opponent 'What would you have done? Taken away his birds?'

A major debating point is scored although a possible rhetorical response might have been to ask 'are you aware of varying levels of punishment in prisons or do you believe them to be all the same?'

False accusation

This is a wicked but sometimes highly effective tactic whereby you accuse your adversary of doing or saying something which *you know to be untrue* and that you are guilty of yourself, either at the time or planning in future. If you are then alleged to have undertaken the same action, respond (without admitting anything) that your opponent did the same thing earlier, as you mentioned.

For example:

Goebbels, the Nazi propagandist allegedly said of Churchill in 1941: *The English follow the principle that when one lies, one should lie big and stick to it. They keep up their lies, even at the risk of looking ridiculous.* This method was precisely that used by Hitler and colleagues to gain support prior to World War II. Had Churchill fought back, then Goebbels would have said that he (Churchill) was just as guilty. Remarkably, in fascist Germany it was found that if a big lie were repeated often enough, the public would come to believe it, just like today when fake news is sometimes believed more readily than authentic news.

Cartoon 3.6

At the time of an election, a corrupt government may make false accusations about the reputation of the opposition and criticise the quality of their candidates. This may backfire as it can create the impression that both sides are equally bad irrespective of the truth.

In a similar manner you could presume something that isn't true and ask people to comment on the consequences. For example:

*'Does the Labour party have less optimism given that they are
likely to lose the forthcoming election in Gateshead?'*

Here is a more recent example related to the war in Ukraine. Russia
accused Ukraine of having a secret chemical and biological
establishment, funded by the USA. The Americans have strongly
denied this but true or not, Russia now considers they are justified in
using their chemical/ biological weapons against Ukraine as it
believed they possessed them. Apart from the false accusation,
possession of such weapons does not imply they will be used. It's as
illogical as accusing a man of adultery just because he has the
apparatus!

How to avoid getting beaten up

Some people like aggressive debate and even a subsequent punch up!
Others need to know when to make a speedy exit unless they are good
at boxing, karate etc. This situation is liable to take place in a pub,
parties or similar social environment where strong feelings may be
fuelled by alcohol and recreational drugs, especially cocaine or meths.

Here are some warning signs ranked by increasing level of danger:

- Your opponent moves closer to you and eye contact is steadfast.
- Their arms are crossed, lips pursed, face flushed, jaw thrust
  forward, nostrils flare, pupils dilate, eyes narrow. Sometimes the
  chest is puffed up and their head is extended slightly.
- A forefinger is raised initially vertically then jabbing towards
  you, emphasizing each word.
- The finger is then poked repeatedly toward or into your chest.
- Blading. This is a change of posture where your opponent faces
  you sideways.
- If indoors, you may be asked to step outside.

Now is the time to run unless you really want a fight!

How to defuse an escalating debate

Look out for the signs of anger listed above and bale out if things are going badly i.e. go outside or leave the room but do not head for the toilet as you may be followed in there and attacked!

Here are a few cooling-off strategies:

- Hunch up, put your chin on the chest and pull your arms close to the body to appear small and submissive
- Say little and listen more
- Try paraphrasing your opponent's point of view in your own language. You might comment: 'so what you are saying is...'
- Change the subject. Use the Straw Man approach as explained earlier in this section
- Hold up both hands about shoulder height and say something like: 'Actually, I think you may be right on that. Perhaps I had mis-understood you.'
- Maybe avoid the word 'sorry', theoretically it should help but in practice it could make matters worse.

CHAPTER 4

MORE SOPHISTICATED METHODS

Extreme it. If you do not like a new idea, take it to the extreme to show (hopefully) that it is unworkable. Here are some examples:

- *Cyclists should be required to register their bicycle and pay third party insurance.* You could oppose this by saying that if every cyclist had to do this, it would be unworkable. The bicycle is the means of transport for the less well-off and such insurance would damage their livelihoods severely. There would be a national revolt.

- *Motorists should be compelled to drive no faster than 20 miles per hour in built up areas.* You might respond by saying 'if everyone behaved like this then traffic would come to a standstill, no-one could get to work, and the economy would collapse'. (London has actually imposed this and so far, there are few problems, apart from speeding fines!)

- *Medical prescriptions should be free irrespective of age and social circumstances.* You could remark that if prescriptions were free for everyone then the Health Services would be bankrupt in no time.

- If it is proposed that some recreational drugs should be decriminalised, the extreme response might be: *'well then, we would have a society of multiple drug addicts, and no-one would do any work'.*

Use Kant logic. This is like the 'extreme' approach. Immanuel Kant proposed a moral principle of 'universalizability' whereby you should act in a way that would be acceptable to all members of society. Here are some examples:

- Should people be allowed to lie on social media? If everyone lied, then there would be no point in communication. If everyone told the truth, then there would be no problem. Therefore, everyone should tell the truth even if some people do not.
- Should people be excused from paying their due taxes? If everyone failed to pay taxes then the government would have a major shortage of income and be less able to support education, health, housing etc. Therefore, everyone should pay taxes.
- Should people be banned from possessing guns? If everyone owned a gun then there would be a risk of illegal use and crime rates would soar. Therefore, gun ownership should be banned.

Reverse causality. Few lay people have heard of this, but it can be a powerful technique to disarm your opponent. Here is an example taken from medicine. It is often stated that head injury may cause subsequent Parkinson's disease (PD). However, people with PD tend to have poor balance early in the disease course and this leads to falls that cause head injury. This brings them into contact with doctors who may note features of PD. There is also the question of *selective recall bias* in that patients are more likely to recall a blow to the head because it is usually a significant event in their life. You could therefore argue that this apparent association is due to *reverse causality* and that it is the disease itself that results in blows to the head rather than the head injury causing the disease. You might also emphasise that *association does not necessarily mean causation*.

In the 1960s many London buses had a conductor whose job was to collect fares and go up and down the stairs as the buses were mostly 'double-deckers'. There was a study of cardiac health in the drivers and conductors where it was noted that the drivers were heavier and tended to have more heart disease and sudden death than the conductors who had a more normal weight (Heady et al 1961). It was inferred that the higher physical activity from climbing up and down stairs by conductors was protective against cardiac disease, whereas the drivers' job was more sedentary and made them susceptible to heart attacks. The association was strong, but it could be argued that separation of drivers and conductors was due to self-selection. Thus, job applicants who were overweight and less fit would choose to be a driver as they might be daunted by the thought of going up and down stairs all day, whereas slimmer and fitter applicants would not be put off by such activities. The popular conclusion was that the low level of job activity in drivers caused excess heart disease, but it could be argued that there may be reversed causality at play, and that the disease (obesity) resulted in self-selection of job preference.

Use reciprocals.

- If raising taxes increase governments' revenues then lowering taxes should decrease them, but in reality, this is not always the case. Sometimes it is found that small tax *reductions* stimulate the economy and result in higher tax returns. See Laffer curves later in this Chapter.

- As a joke: 'Most people only need to shower once per week. People who shower every day must be dirty'.

- If fat people allegedly do not eat, then thin people must eat too much.

- Increasing the time spent in prison will only result in overcrowding so we should reduce the duration of sentences.

- If someone states that all cosmetics containing synthetic ingredients are *bad* on the basis of one such sample, then would they assume that all cosmetics containing natural ingredients are *good* on the basis of just one sample? The same argument could be applied to vaccines and their side effects.

- If you owe a firm a large sum of money by a certain date and you find it difficult to pay back, you might offer to reimburse by instalments. If the firm say it is against their regulations, you might respond my stating there is nothing in their rules to say you should <u>not</u> pay by instalments. Their rules may be *implicit but* not *explicit.*

Cartoon 4.1

Shout out single words or peoples' names to distract your opponent.

Smart people will get the point, but it might disrupt their train of thought. The full name or just the surname may suffice to distract.

For example, blurt out:

Emmeline Pankhurst: in reference to women's rights debates.

Karl Marx: if the conversation seems to be favouring a socialist proposal that you do not like.

Enoch Powell: the politician notorious for supporting a ban on Black immigrants. You could also mention the phrase 'Rivers of blood' which refers to one of his infamous speeches against immigration (1968).

Tolpuddle: The martyrs who campaigned for workers' rights.

Frankenstein: Useful when there is concern about unregulated genetic engineering - for plants, humans etc.

Mandy Rice-Davies: Famous for her phrase 'Well, he would, wouldn't he'. This was in response to a question in court about her alleged affair with Lord Astor who denied having any such relationship.

The 'I have a right' argument. Human rights are enshrined in the Human Rights Act (HRA, 1998) and it is perfectly acceptable to cite sections from that. Despite this, many people state they have a 'right' to almost anything irrespective of the HRA. For example:

- I have a right to smoke in a restaurant and for as long as I want
- If I wish to walk in the middle of the road that is within my rights
- I have a right to park my car wherever I wish without incurring a fine
- I have a right not to wear a car seat belt even though it is against the law
- I have a right to roam the countryside wherever I wish to go

Chewbacca defence. This is a strategy with some similarity to the *Straw Man* defence. It can be used to infer that because an event or piece of information is extremely unlikely it is therefore false. Chewbacca is the 8-foot Wookie in Star Wars who allegedly wanted to live on Endor wherein reside the 2-foot tall Ewoks. This is unbelievable but the trick is to compare this situation with the main focus of a debate and infer *that* is, likewise, implausible. Just because one situation is unlikely does not mean that another is just as implausible. Despite the clear absence of logic, this defence strategy has the potential to fool opponents and juries, so watch out! It was used with success, in the defence of OJ Simpson who was accused of a double murder in 1994

Cartoon 4.2

The Gish Gallop. This is a debating ploy that aims to overwhelm an opponent with as many points as possible, regardless of their validity. It is named after Duane Gish, a biochemist who favoured a literal interpretation of the book of Genesis. If you are subjected to the Gish Gallop your defence might be to say:

- 'I'm not sure I follow all of that perhaps you could repeat your main question/point'

The 80:20 rule. This is more guidance than a hard and fast rule, but it can be a very powerful debating tool. For example, if there is a system of social benefit payments for single mothers, one might assume that 80% will use the system fairly; 10% will abuse it and make false claims and 10% will be ignorant of the benefit or too proud to make a claim. One can set a 'moral compass' to decide whether an 80:20 split is acceptable, or should it be 90:10 or 70:30? This debating instrument does of course need to be supported by reliable data. A common statement is:

- I think that those people on benefits are all scroungers (or 'Chavs') who have never done a decent day's work in their life.

You could well respond that there are indeed benefit cheats, but they represent a minority and that is balanced by those who are entitled to claim but do not, for a variety of reasons. As mentioned, you must have good figures available to support your stance.

Divide and Rule. Apart from yourself, there needs to be at least two others present, ideally experts. If the topic is contentious, it is unlikely that the experts will agree completely. If you do not like the advice/conclusions by the experts, the trick is to steer the conversation into the contentious areas, highlight points of disagreement and say something like:

- 'if you two experts cannot agree on this matter then how can anyone possibly form a plausible opinion?'

In politics this approach may be used to weaken the power of opponents. See mock debate numbers 10 and 14.

Constructive ambiguity. This is the deliberate use of ambiguous language in debate. It was popular with Henry Kissinger (former US Secretary of State) who employed this method to give people on both sides of a dispute the feeling they have achieved something, thus avoiding humiliation. After the Yom Kippur war (1973), Kissinger constructed the following paragraph. It was deliberately vague and interpreted in different ways by Arabs and Israelis.

> 'Both sides agree that discussions between them will begin immediately to settle the question of the return to the October 22 positions in the framework of agreement on the disengagement and separation of forces under the auspices of the UN.'

Here is another in which the actual phrase is used!

> 'In order to draft mandates which are to form the basis for consensus, a key element is required: constructive ambiguity, namely, to enable the Conference to reach a major decision while postponing agreement on difficult details to a later, more focused stage.'

This technique is still applied in the belief that it keeps opposing parties around the negotiating table and sustains the hope that meaningful agreement will be reached eventually.

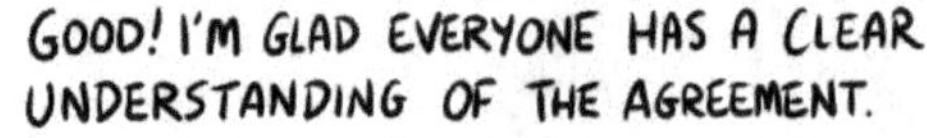

Cartoon 4.3

Beware the tendency to dichotomise. In other words, take heed of topics that are classed as good or bad; just or unjust.

> 'Vitamins are good for you, therefore not taking vitamins must be unhealthy.'

Inevitably this will lead to the conclusion often favoured by manufacturers that consuming more vitamins will benefit your health even further.

According to Mae West the famous American actress:

> 'If a little is great, and a lot is better, then way too much is just about right!'

Introduce sophisticated concepts that your opposite member might not be familiar with.

- *Horseshoe theory* in political debate. This highlights the notion of similarities between widely differing viewpoints. Thus, anti-Semitic views or actions may be displayed by those belonging to far left *and* far right-wing parties. Both may employ violent means to further their ends.
- *Nudge theory.* This refers to a means of influencing behaviour without obvious coercion. The inventors (Thaler and Sunstein, 2009) term this 'paternalistic libertarianism'. For example, if fruit in a shop is placed next to the cash-till then people are more likely to make a purchase than if it is elsewhere. When people in the UK were sent reminders about their tax arrears, the level of payment increased when the wording was changed to '9 out of 10 people in your area are up to date with their tax payments'. It may be useful to cite or apply nudge theory when discussing *Rules vs Standards*. A rule could be a road speed limit. If you drive faster than say, 30 miles per hour then you will have broken a rule and will probably suffer a penalty. Alternatively, the same stretch of road could have a notice saying 'please keep your speed down below 30 mph'; 'please drive considerately' or a sign that displays your speed if it is above 30 mph.

Cartoon 4.4

- ***Broken window theory.*** This is an idea conceived by criminologists Wilson and Kelling, that if someone breaks a window and it is not fixed quickly then that acts as an acceptance signal to commit further increasingly violent acts. It is used to support the concept of 'zero tolerance' in policing.

- ***Sliding doors moment.*** The term goes back to the 1998 movie 'Sliding Doors' where Helen Quilley played by Gwyneth Paltrow in one scenario, just manages to open the carriage doors on a London underground train with consequent events. In the other scenario she is too late and the carriage doors close. In general, it refers to a seemingly unimportant incident or comment that subsequently has major consequences. In JB Priestley's famous play 'Dangerous Corner' a chance remark by a guest, triggers a series of devastating revelations including secret relationships that have tragic consequences.

- ***Catastrophe theory.*** This was originally a mathematical modelling term to describe loss of stability in a dynamic system, but it has escaped into lay parlance to describe how systems in society or in Nature have intrinsic weaknesses that ultimately cause them to fail abruptly. This theory has been used to describe the development of major wars such as World War I and II. Related to this are the:

- o *Butterfly effect.* This is an idea embodied in the closely related *Chaos Theory* that small events can have a massive impact on a complex system. A popular example is that of a butterfly flapping its wings in New Mexico causing a hurricane in China.

- o *Tipping point.* This is the notion proposed by Malcolm Gladwell in his book (The Tipping Point) that small actions at the right time in the right place with the right people can create a tipping moment. This can be a product, idea, or trend. It is basically a threshold concept. Once the tipping point crosses a threshold it then spreads rapidly. Morton Grodzins, the sociologist, studied American neighbourhoods in the early 1960s and often found that the relative number of Black families remained small. When 'one too many' Black families arrived, the tipping point was reached, and the remaining white families moved out *en masse*

- o *Perfect storm.* A combination of unfavourable events leading to disaster. Often applied to economics to predict a stock market crash. It is like the phrase 'a recipe for disaster'.

- *Moral Algebra.* This is an approach to debating and discovery of the truth, which harks back to Benjamin Franklin who probably defined it first in 1772. In brief, the points in favour of a particular idea are listed and each given an arbitrary numerical score. Then the opposing arguments are registered and scored likewise. When the points for and against are added together, the idea/motion that scores highest should be the best answer.

- *Theory of Mind.* In brief, this concept refers to the ability of someone to guess what another person thinks or feels. Women are slightly better at this than men. People with autism are particularly poor at this and to lesser degree those with the closely related, Asperger's syndrome. You might wish to bring up this theory into debate, perhaps to point out that someone whose views you oppose, are unable to perceive the effects of their actions or beliefs on others. Related to this, is the concept:

We may be better at seeing the flaws in other people's thinking than our own.

This concept could be applied in debate in an attempt to weaken an opponent's view.

- **Karl Popper approach.** The debate starts with a proposal which is then falsified. The classical example is the statement 'all swans are white' which is generally true. When someone found black swans in Australia, this observation was falsified. When there are no more known falsehoods, then what is left, in theory at least, should be the truth! It was introduced originally to address methods of seeking the truth in science and philosophy but may be applied to many areas of knowledge.

Cartoon 4.5

Here is a theoretical but valid debate relevant to medicine:

Most people with headaches have a brain tumour.

Given that is true, is there anything that might suggest this is false?

They may have migraine or tension headache instead.

Given that most people with headache may just have migraine or tension headache, is there anything else that would make you think that such people did not have a brain tumour?

A brain scan may be normal.

Given that brain scans are usually normal in this context, and that most peoples' headaches are due to migraine or tension headache, could the patient still have a brain tumour?

Yes. If the scan had a CT scan because the sensitivity for brain tumours is lower for growths in the posterior fossa (base of the brain). An MRI brain scan would be better.

Given that the MRI brain scans are nearly always normal in this situation and that most patients with headache have migraine or tension headache is there anything else that might change the diagnosis?

No, I would be happy that an MRI brain scan would exclude the possibility of a brain tumour and that most people with headache do not have a brain tumour.

Thus, the premise that 'most people with headaches have a brain tumour' is progressively falsified. This approach has been used for medical diagnostic purposes, but it would be a bit dull in ordinary conversation!

- ***Occam's Razor.*** This states that if there are multiple possible causes for an event then the one with the fewest assumptions, the simplest, is likely the correct one. It is sometimes applied to medicine where a patient may have several disorders say, resulting in a stroke (high blood pressure, diabetes, obesity, raised cholesterol, heart disease, bad family history) but the real cause is just one of these, such as high blood pressure.

The opposite view is **Hickam's dictum:** *'a patient can have as many diseases as he darn well pleases'.*

- ***Social evolutionary theory.*** This can be useful when the debate revolves around hostile political regimes. You may wish to quote Montesquieu, the 18th century French philosopher who proposed an evolutionary scheme consisting of three stages: hunting or savagery, herding or barbarism, and civilization. The concept could be applied for example, in discussions over brutal dictatorships where the rest of the world moralises or just stands by. You could respond by agreeing with the facts but pointing out that through the process of social evolution, such dictatorships are gradually replaced with more benign regimes, although it may take a long time (several hundred years in the case of the UK!). If you need a quip you might say:

  'The USA is the only country that passed from barbarism to decadence without the intervention of civilisation!'

- ***Socratic Jujitsu.*** This is a term coined by Jennifer Hancock in 2017. It is a subtle approach that is well worth understanding and mentioned briefly above. If you are starting a discussion and your opponent appears to agree with you – beware – you may be under attack! Your adversary is likely to be an experienced debater. Unless you are careful, your beliefs may be demolished piece by piece and before you know it, you will have lost and unable to understand why. See Cartoon 2.1 and debate number 7.

- ***Laffer Curves.*** This concept is applied mainly to taxation. In theory, the higher the rate of taxation, the greater the revenue for the government. However there comes a point when raising taxes actually reduces income (reminiscent of the 'tipping point' as above). The motivation to work becomes less and bosses spend more time trying to minimise tax payment. A graph of income raised against tax rate is like a mountainous peak as in Figure 4.1.

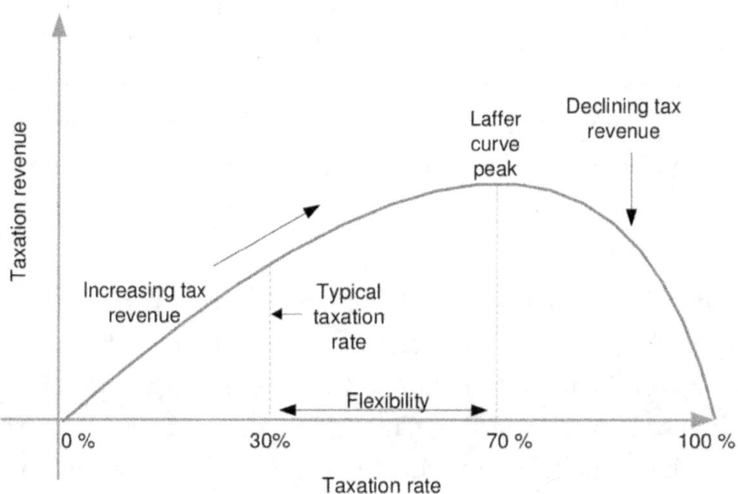

Figure 4.1. The Laffer curve. Hypothetical relationship between taxation revenue (or Gross Domestic Product) plotted against taxation rate. Figure reproduced with permission from Lees KR (2013)

Cartoon 4.6

The same principle can be applied to efficiency in commerce. The more savings and good organization a firm makes, then the greater its profits will be – up to a point. Further efficiencies can make a firm less profitable as there is loss of flexibility, and this can lead to bankruptcy.

In health care, all practising clinicians need medical protection insurance to assist with malpractice claims – especially for high-risk specialities like obstetrics, gynaecology, or cosmetic surgery. Greater protection may create a demand for more lawyers to implement the changes and defend against any litigation. There may come a point whereby the cost of such insurance makes it uneconomical for surgeons to practice.

In London and in many other large cities there is a fee for driving into central areas – the 'congestion charge'. If there is still too much traffic and problems with pollution from car exhausts then someone may suggest, quite logically, that the congestion charge – currently £15 per day – should be raised. The increased income could then be used to improve traffic and pedestrian safety etc. However, motorists may find the raised fee unacceptably high and use other forms of transport, resulting in reduced revenue and no improvement in proposed safety measures. This is, once more, a threshold concept that mirrors the 'Tipping Point' explained earlier.

- The Dunning-Kruger effect. This goes back to two social psychologists who in 1999 described 'illusionary superiority'. It refers to those who are unskilled yet unaware of their incompetence and have an inflated view of their own abilities. A form of hubris really. The opposite is a cognitive bias in which people who do excel tend to *under*-estimate their own ability whilst over-estimating such qualities in others. In college examinations some low performers may over-estimate their scores whereas high performers may think they did worse than reality. It has been highlighted recently in the Covid epidemic, where articulate non-experts with no scientific credentials have disagreed with epidemiologists and virologists typically on social media often to oppose the use of vaccines.

CHAPTER 5

STATISTICS

DO NOT SKIP THIS CHAPTER! If you wish to succeed in debate, you ABSOLUTELY MUST know this chapter back to front. It has been simplified as much as possible and hopefully should be easy to understand.

Statistics are probably the most frequently abused element of any conversation. If you do not like your adversaries' use of statistics try one of these strategies:

- As Benjamin Disraeli once said 'there are three kinds of lies: lies, damn lies and statistics.

Or simply:

- You can prove anything by use of statistics.

- Read the book by Darrel Huff (1993) titled "How to Lie with Statistics"

Not all statistics or statistical presentations are lies. What debaters need, is how to distinguish manipulated truths from the real truth.

In the field of new medical therapies, Big Pharma are alleged to go to inordinate lengths to make their new product appear beneficial and attain approval from the relevant regulatory authority. You may find this hard to believe but for example, just try to access the raw data concerning a trial of a new medication. Numerous obstacles will be put in your way. It's not just Pharma, even doctors with no industry ties may be reluctant to disclose their raw data. The amount paid to clinical staff for lectures or 'consultancies' etc. may be revealing. Some of this is publicly available and may be viewed in Propublica (for USA) and ABPI (for UK). Money, ego and fame seduce both Pharma and academics. If this area interests you, the book to read is 'Bad Pharma' by Ben Goldacre (2014).

Cartoon 5.1

Despite all this, you are unlikely to succeed in many conversations without a basic grasp of statistical principles and I make no apology for a very fundamental explanation of some of the strengths and weaknesses of this much maligned science.

You need to become familiar with graphs and their attributes. The 'X' axis or 'abscissa' is the same as the horizontal axis. The 'Y' axis or 'ordinate' is the same as the vertical axis. Thus in debate:

it's a good ploy to talk about the X and Y axis or abscissa and ordinate respectively as there is a reasonable chance your opponent may not know the difference or mix them up.

The 'Normal' (Gaussian, Bell-shaped) Distribution

Study Figure 5.1 (left) below. The curve is symmetrical, shaped like a bell and shows an idealised model about the frequency of values observed and is known as a 'Normal' distribution of data. The measurements can represent almost anything: height, weight, number of cars, number of children etc. In a given population which has a Normal scatter of results, about two-thirds of people (68.27% to be exact) will have a value scattered symmetrically around the centre point, which is known as the Mean or Average. Individuals whose data fall within this central, two-thirds group, are said to have a value within one standard deviation (SD) of the mean. 95% of the population have a value within two standard deviations and virtually everyone (99.7%) falls within the 3 SD limit.

The peak of a Normal curve is also called the Mode and represents *the most frequently observed value*. It is exactly the same as the Mean but *only if the curve is Normal*. The Median is the mid-point of all values and in a Normal curve it has the same value as the Mean.

Thus, in a Normal curve the mean, median and mode all have the same value. Figure 5.1 (right) shows the heights of individuals on the horizontal axis and their numbers on the vertical axis. There are two Normally distributed curves, here for height, in women and men. Most women in this sample are on average 164 cm tall.

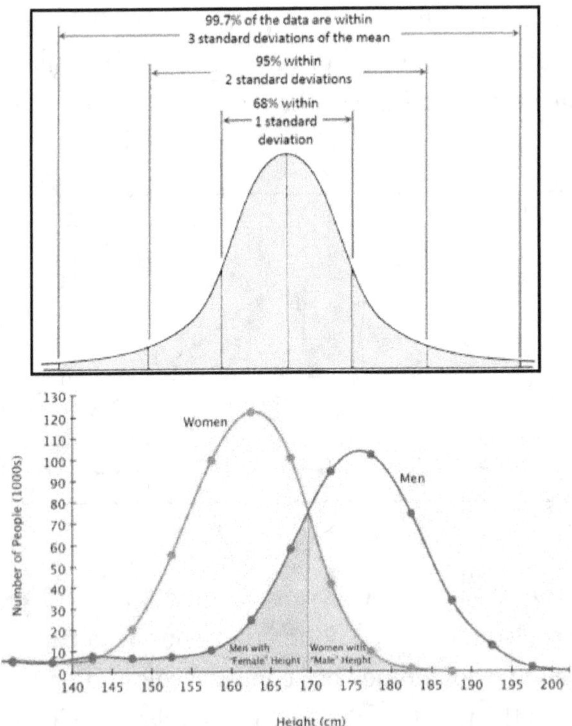

Figure 5.1. Left: the 'Normal' (Gaussian, bell-shaped) distribution of data coloured blue. The peak is known as the mean, average, median or mode depending on its shape. In a Normal curve all have the same value. Reproduced from Dan Kernler - CC BY-SA 4.0. https://commons.wikimedia.org/w/index.php?curid=36506025.

Right: Normal curves for height of men and women. If the item is Normally distributed then you could say that having a height of 164cm is *normal* for a female and extreme deviations (third SD) from this would be *abnormal*, such as being excessively tall at 183cm or very short at 142cm. Reproduced from Google Images.

Sometimes the distribution of values is not Normal as in Figure 5.2. The peak of the curve is called the Mode, as it represents the most frequently observed value. The Median is the mid-point of all values and in this example, the mean or average is to the right as shown. This curve might represent incomes, with a few on the far right earning large sums while most (the Mode) earn modest amounts.

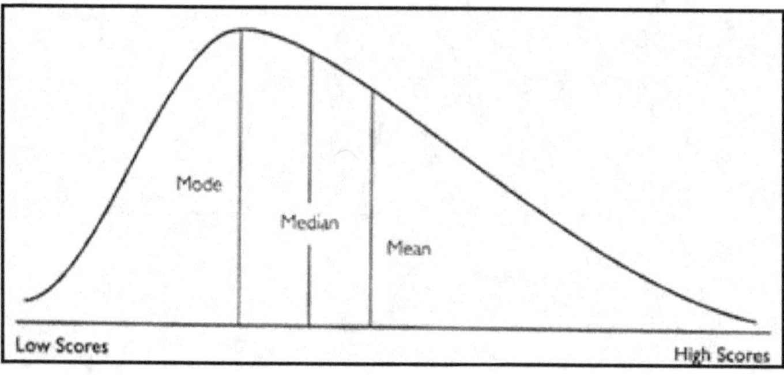

Figure 5.2. A non-Normal 'skewed' distribution. The 'Mean' or 'Average' is the sum of observations (here on the vertical axis) on the graph divided by the number of people (here on the horizontal axis). The 'Median' is the middle value and the 'Mode' is the most frequently observed value as shown. Reproduced from Google Images.

Most people use the term 'Average' to indicate the Mean, which is correct, but others use Average alternatively and often deviously, to indicate the Mode or Median. It is clearly important to agree on the definition being used, given the wide distance of values between the Mode and Mean as shown in Figure 5.2.

In debate watch out for the flexible use of the term 'Average' and ask which of the three definitions of 'Average' is being applied.

Although the underlying principles of normal distribution etc. are taught at school, it is often understood poorly by adults, thus knowledge of the Bell Curve, means, medians and modes are prerequisites for arguments. Learn these principles and then apply them ruthlessly in debate! It can be so easy to confuse your opponent unless they have some grounding in statistical methods, and many will not.

Use the term 'Aggregate'. In the domain of statistics this means that most people would share a particular viewpoint. This could be defined as having a value falling within one standard deviation. It is a useful counter-attack for anecdotes as explained below. In democracies it is rarely possible to satisfy much more than 50% of the population, thus arguing for an extreme point of view will rarely be productive. Hence:

- *Death penalty for first degree murder.* The aggregate response for many Western countries (apart from some states in USA) would be against this suggestion. (See debate number 9).
- *Decriminalising use of cannabis.* Again, the aggregate opinion is likely to be in favour of this

You could equally well argue that the term majority should apply only to 51% or more (or minority of 49% or less). In either instance the terms (majority, aggregate etc.) should be agreed and followed by hard facts and figures to prove your case.

Here someone quotes an anecdote:

- *I think we should have stricter religious and moral education in schools. I knew one pupil who became radicalised at the age of 14 years and went to fight for ISIS in Syria.*

You might respond:

- 'Your example is purely of anecdotal significance and likely an extreme viewpoint held by a very small percentage of people, well outside the third standard deviation as I'm sure you will understand (hoping that they do not and that they are unable to produce reliable figures).

- In a vaccination debate someone will usually oppose vaccines and say something like 'I know a lady whose child had the 6-in-one vaccine (diphtheria, hepatitis B, influenza, polio, tetanus and whooping cough). Her child then developed seizures and never did well at school'. This argument should be countered by citing the risk of seizures resulting from the vaccine (about 1:10,000), compared to the expected incidence of epilepsy from other causes in the same period in those who did not receive the vaccine (about 5:10,000).

Alternatively, you could use the 'reciprocal attack' and state 'how likely would you be to approve a new medicine on the basis of a single successful dose?'

Ask for tests of significance

Always ask how likely an observation is the result of the play of chance or not. A well-known explanation of this comes from the British statistician, Ronald Fisher, where he asks how could you test if a woman really can tell if milk is added into the tea or whether the tea is poured onto the milk? You could test this by supplying five different cups of milky tea and ask how they were prepared. Since there are only two alternatives (tea in first or milk in first) by chance she would be right 50% at each attempt assuming she had no such ability. This is written as 50/50; 1:2 or ½. The likelihood of identifying *all 5 cups* correctly by pure guesswork is calculated by multiplying the sequential risks: ½ x ½ x ½ x ½ x ½ = 1/32 or 0.03. This tells us that someone *without* the ability to discriminate how the tea was prepared might still get it right but only once in every 32 tries. This is a small probability to occur by chance and could persuade us that someone probably does have the ability to tell how the tea was prepared if they got it right each time.

This figure of 0.03 (or 1:32) is the *p value* or probability value. It is basically a measure of how likely an observation has occurred by the play of chance or not. By convention, statistical significance for a *non-chance* observation is set at 1 in 20 (1:20) or smaller – such as 1:40. Thus:

> For an occurrence at 1:20 the p value is: p=0.05 (just significant and against pure chance)

> For an occurrence at 1:50 the p value is: p=0.02 (significant)

> For an occurrence at 1:1000 the p value is: p=0.001 (highly significant)

> For an occurrence at 1:10 the p value is: p=0.10 (not significant and consistent with a chance finding)

If you toss a 6-sided dice ('die' in the USA) then the chance of throwing a six is 1:6. If you threw three 6's in a row, the odds of this happening are 1/6 x 1/6 x 1/6 = 1/216 (p=0.005). If this happened in reality, then you were incredibly lucky, or the dice was loaded!

The above is a major simplification of statistical probability but if you grasp the principles, you will be able to pulverise most opponent's even if you can't do all the calculations.

Cartoon 5.2

Use the term 'Case-Mix'. In some regions there are large numbers of elderly people or those living in overcrowded circumstances, all on low incomes making high demands on local health care services. Other areas may be more affluent and make fewer requests. Clearly, it is not valid to allocate financial resources based purely on gross population numbers. Funding should be adjusted according to needs and the population *case-mix*. Despite this, some regions appear to receive financial resources according to political party affiliation especially for 'swing' areas, where the vote may oscillate between say, Labour and Conservative (UK) or Republican and Democratic parties (USA) in national elections. In another situation, two hospitals might wish to assess their outcomes. It can be misleading to compare one hospital that handled rare complex diseases with another hospital that dealt with more frequent problems. The first hospital might have surgeons who are skilled at second or third revision cardiac bypass operations where scarring and prior bypasses make surgery more difficult. The likelihood of post-operative complications would be higher and length of stay greater than a less specialised hospital. In this instance, case-mix would address the imbalance by comparing those undergoing their *first* bypass in both units and those having a *revised* procedure in either centre. It needs to be a 'like with like' comparison.

Use the term 'Case-Control Study'. It often helps to know whether certain groups in society are the same or different with respect to e.g., a given disease. The people with the illness are the 'cases' and those without it are the 'controls'. It is important that the cases and controls should be as near identical as possible apart from the condition under study, which in this instance, is illness. Thus, the cases and controls should consist of the same age group, ethnicity, income band, size of house, number of children etc. Although desirable, in reality, it is not always possible to achieve perfect matching of cases and controls, and some compromises have to be made.

In the Covid-19 pandemic it was noted that UK Afro-Caribbean and other minority groups were dying from the disease more frequently than Whites. The crude death rate was 4.2 times higher. However, it is known that Afro-Caribbean and other ethnic minorities often live in socially deprived areas, have lower incomes, have less favourable living accommodation and a greater number of co-existing illnesses ('co-morbidities'). When the data were adjusted for all measured variables, so that the cases and controls (Afro-Caribbean and Whites) were as near identical as possible, it was found that the risk of death in Afro-Caribbean compared to Whites dropped from 4.2 times to 1.9. There was still an unexplained amount of excess mortality in Afro-Caribbean but far less than the crude 4.2-fold increase in death observed originally. One official stated that the rate in Afro-Caribbean was 90% higher (1.9 vs 1.0) – which is correct for a *relative* difference, but the *absolute* difference is 0.9 i.e. just under one person more in every 100.

In the above example, the true rate for Afro-Caribbean could in fact be *no different* or even higher for *Whites*, especially where the sample sizes are small. All such information will have an inaccuracy or *margin of error* depending on how carefully the sample (people, diseases, incomes etc) was obtained and matched. In essence, the true value could be higher or lower than the figure cited.

'Margin of error'. This is measured typically by one of three indices: standard deviation (SD), standard error (SE) and a closely related index, the confidence interval (CI). As mentioned above, one SD contains about two thirds of the data around the mean (see Figure 5.1). The lower the SD the more likely the data are accurate, and this may be suspected if the shape of the curve is narrow and peaked. The SE is a measure of how much the Mean varies around the true value when there are repeated observations, and it is expressed as +/- 1 SE. For example, a small town might record a mean of 125,600 car owners one year, but the total will vary from one year to the next. If the SE is found to be 300, the range of estimates would be 125,300-125,900 car owners. Clearly, the smaller the sample size the larger the SE and the less reliable the estimate would be. The most reliable data have very small SEs.

In debate, where someone mentions a basic number as above, it is important to ask for the margin of error. If this information is lacking it is likely their figure is either unreliable or for various reasons, not obtainable.

Finally, the confidence interval (CI) indicates a range of values that is likely to contain the true value. In the above example, the Mean might be 125,600 car owners with a lower CI of 120,000 and the upper CI of 131,200. This is expressed as 125,600 (95% CI: 120,000 to 131,200).

Rarely mentioned in media debate are margins of error or indeed *any* tests to determine whether such values are significantly different from each other.

Cartoon 5.3

Thus, the *case-control* method is a powerful technique that quantifies the principle of comparing like with like. Whenever it is suggested that certain social groups tend to behave differently (more crime, possession of knives, more traffic violations, more children etc.)

always ask for case-control evidence. Regularly such statements are based on casual observations or data that are unadjusted for variables such as social class, education, ethnicity, income etc. as explained above.

'Observed and Expected Data'. The above examples belong to the category of *observed vs expected findings.* Diseases, accidents, unpleasant events occur all the time, thus it is important to determine whether a particular event happened by chance or not. This information may be obtained through records of weather, serious illnesses, road traffic accidents etc. In medicine, the standard approach when assessing new medication is to use a dummy (placebo) group compared to those on the real compound (active group). Basically, this is a specific type of case–control study or 'randomised trial'.

Here is an example. Say a promising new drug for migraine has been discovered. Researchers may wish to try it out on a large number of people, say 1,000 who will need to have experienced at least two migraine attacks per month ('inclusion criteria'). Ideally, all participants should be as near identical as possible: of similar age, gender, social and ethnic category etc. Then, at the start of the trial, half are given, at random, either the active medication or placebo. It is important that neither the patient nor any staff concerned with the trial are aware what type of medication a patient is taking – active or placebo. This is called a 'double-blind' trial because none of the people undertaking the trial, including medical staff will know who is taking the real drug. The random allocation to active drug or placebo provides an unbiased assignment to one or other treatment arm (active drug or placebo) without any prior indication about who might do better on the active drug. If the *observed* number of migraine attacks in the active medication group is significantly less than *expected* when compared to the placebo group, then the drug is probably effective.

Significance is defined by the *p value* as detailed above.

You might ask, why is a placebo group needed? Why not just give the active medication to everyone? The answer is that many trial volunteers improve when given placebo. In the case of migraine, it is known that at least 30% of volunteers given placebo will experience fewer attacks. So, any new medication for migraine must beat 30% by a significant margin – measured, of course, by the p value!

This principle can be applied in many other disciplines. Say there was concern about the number of traffic accidents in a particular town and it was proposed to lower the speed limit from 30 miles/hour to 20 miles/hour. The number of accidents and their severity in the speed-restricted area could be compared to another near identical section of road over, say, one year and the differences compared. In education, this method could be applied to classroom pupil sizes. In politics, to the effects of competing campaign strategies. Despite the compelling logic, this approach is applied infrequently.

BIAS

There is risk of bias in everyday observations, but it is of major importance in politics and in the scientific domain especially for case-control studies. Twelve biases are discussed here, but there are many others.

a) **Selective recall bias.** You have a birthday in April and that day it pours with rain. You might want to say 'it always rains on my birthday' but it might be just selective recall of rainy days. To prove this was true you would need to check weather records for your entire lifetime and document how many days it rained on that day and where you were on your birthday. You would then need to apply statistical tests to determine whether the rainfall figure on that day differed significantly from chance. You would finish with a p value as explained above.

Here is another example: 'men with a moustache are always aggressive'. This observation might relate to personal experience or knowledge of historical figures such as Hitler, Stalin, or Franco all of whom wore a moustache. To prove this link would require for example, the collection of several hundreds of people with moustaches, but no beards (the cases) matched to other identical people except for having no moustache (the controls). Then a personality profile would have to be administered to both groups to determine if there was a statistically significant difference between them. To my knowledge this has not been done!

Selective recall bias is clearly a weak debating ploy akin to anecdotes, nonetheless it is used extensively and needs to be pounced on immediately with a request for hard factual and statistical evidence.

Cartoon 5.4

b) Myside, Confirmation Bias and Conflict of Interest. This is the tendency to put forward arguments that only support your viewpoint while holding back any opinion to the contrary.

For example, someone who did not believe in climate change might say:

There is not a shred of evidence in support of climate change, it just represents natural variation in the normal oscillations of world temperature that produces hot and cold spells. There was a 'warm period' in the 13th century wasn't there? (true, actually). What caused that? Climate change is just another mad idea from looney left pacifists in sandals and smelly socks.

There could well be a *conflict of interest* that has influenced this climate change denier plus pigeon-holing/stereotyping of opposing groups (also see debate number 4). You will not get far with an opponent like this unless you have a firm grasp of available facts and figures.

Many high-profile businessmen believe there is no point in trading with African countries as they are all 'developing' and have low incomes. As pointed out by Hans Rosling in his book, 'Factfulness' (2019), there are at least five prosperous African countries (Tunisia, Algeria, Morocco, Libya and Egypt). Developing trade links with them (and probably many others) could be a lucrative long-term investment.

In courts of law there can be major Myside Bias. Although rarely stated, both prosecuting and defending barristers (trial attorneys in USA) are usually out to win. Their reputations are at stake and ultimately their earning capacity. A lawyer who wins only occasionally is unlikely to attract further clients. This potential conflict may affect the professional conduct of less scrupulous barristers and result in deliberate withholding of relevant evidence, over-use of leading questions, over-emphasis on hearsay evidence ('verbiage'), aggressive cross-examination of witnesses, secret video-recordings of client activities etc. An astute judge may well see through all this, but a jury may not and as a result they could be influenced unduly.

Remember to probe for conflict of interest. This is rarely divulged unless the individual is pressed. Politicians are supposed to register their business interests, but it is unusual for them to declare such conflicts unless they are specifically asked. See debate number 5 on climate change.

c) **Sampling bias.** As detailed above, the two or more groups in a case-control sample should be as near equal as possible. If not, errors will occur. At the polling station for an election, people are often asked how they voted – the 'exit poll'. This sample would not include postal votes thus the two samples – counted votes / exit poll votes - will be unmatched. The 'omitted variable' namely the postal vote, will not have been included thus compromising any conclusion.

d) **Self-serving Bias.** In surveys, when volunteers are asked for their opinion on topics that might conflict with the interviewer's employer, this tends not to be mentioned or downplayed. For example, if there is a question about the volunteer's ability in maths or driving a car, the answers are likely to be overstatements of the truth. Political campaigns are notorious for devising surveys with wording that is biased towards their point of view. For example, 'do you support Ms Smith who rightly states that fairness in elections should override making more polling stations available'. This is a circular argument as well.

Here is a mock questionnaire drawn from 'Yes Minister' that will tend to secure a vote *in favour of* introducing National Service (conscription):

1. Are you worried about the number of young people without jobs?
2. Are you worried about the rise in crime among teenagers?
3. Do you think there is lack of discipline in our comprehensive schools?
4. Do you think young people welcome some authority and leadership in their lives?
5. Do you think they'll respond to a challenge?
6. Would you be in favour of reintroducing National Service?

An alternative questionnaire can be rigged to produce the opposite vote, i.e. *against* the introduction of National Service.

1. Are you worried about the danger of war?
2. Are you worried about the growth of armaments?
3. Do you think there's a danger in giving young people guns and teaching them how to kill?
4. Do you think it's wrong to force people to take up arms against their will?
5. Would you oppose the reintroduction of National Service?

e) **Experimenter Expectation Bias.** If the purpose of a questionnaire based, case-control survey is known to those carrying it out, then the answers from participants will tend to reflect the preconceptions of the person administering the questionnaire. For example, if a study relates to the presence of racism in schools, and the individual administering it is a white person who believes there is no such prejudice, the results are likely to show little racial discrimination.

f) **Noise bias.** This relates to a concept described by Kahneman et al (2021) in their book 'Noise, A Flaw in Human Judgment'. In essence, they highlight the variability and errors between professionals undertaking identical work. This applies particularly to doctors making a pathological diagnosis on identical specimens, judges who issue different sentences for identical crimes and wide-ranging insurance premium rates recommended by underwriters. This concept could be useful in debate where you may wish to challenge an alleged expert. You should also be familiar with the concept of 'margin of error' as discussed in the statistics section above.

g) **Status Quo Bias.** The tendency to leave things as they are. Don't rock the boat. 'If it's not broken don't fix it'. See also the 'Panglossian fallacy' (Chapter 2).

h) **Blind Spot Bias (Bias blind spot).** Some people are able to recognise the effect of bias in others but not in themselves. Many clinicians receive gifts or meals from Big Pharma. This can and does exert subtle pressure to use the medication promoted by the donating company. Clinicians with blind spot bias deny this has any effect on their prescribing habits although they may be well aware of the effect of such donations on their colleagues.

i) **Availability bias (Availability heuristic).** This refers to a tendency of people to make decisions based on readily available anecdotes or well-presented stories on TV or social media instead of seeking scientifically based information. Just because an idea or fact is readily available does not make it any more valuable. For example, if there has been a recent plane crash, some people will develop increased fear of flying. This is irrational, as the risks of flight accidents is extremely low but because a crash happens to be topical this bias is foremost in peoples' thoughts. If the weather is unusually cold for a few weeks, then extremists will use this information to deny climate change.

j) **Action bias.** This is the tendency to do *something* rather than *nothing.* If patients with cancer are given a choice of a 10% risk of death from surgery compared to a 5% risk of doing nothing, they chose surgery (Fagerlin et al 2005). In football, where there is a penalty shootout, goalkeepers tend to leap to one side, despite the fact that many studies show the best approach is to stay put in the centre of the goal (Bar-Eli et al 2007).

k) **Regression to the mean.** This refers to a tendency for initial measurements to be inaccurate but when re-measured they become closer to the mean/average value. For example, the average blood pressure in healthy young people is around 120/70. Say you measure blood pressure at the same time and place every week in 100 people. At the start there will be some high (175/110) or low (110/65) readings usually termed 'outliers'. This often happens because of variables, like how the person is feeling, whether they were in a hurry, had difficulty parking etc. Outliers are more likely to be called back for re-measurement. With repeated assessment, the readings become more representative and accurate. Extreme values tend to disappear and get closer to the mean value. People unaware of this phenomenon may report that numerous people have high or low blood pressures, based (incorrectly) on their initial observations. Regression to the mean is an important bias that plagues small samples and leads the unwary into mis-interpretation of their results.

This phenomenon also occurs in sport. A new footballer might score 20 goals over the season and looks like a sensation. In the next year, the player's goal total may still be good but usually drops slightly because the first season was 'lucky' and that extreme run of goals is unlikely to be repeated.

l) **Publication bias.** This is the tendency to publish results that are only positive i.e. those that support a particular theory or show benefit of a particular medication or other course of treatment. Most researchers find negative results uninteresting, and they are reluctant to publish them. Despite this, it is generally agreed that a negative result is just as valuable scientifically as a positive one and such publications are encouraged.

Use the term percentiles rather than percentages.

So many well-educated people do not know the difference.

Percentage is a number out of 100. It allows comparison between groups of different sizes. Thus, 10% could mean 10 out of 100; 20 out of 200 or 35 out of 350. It can refer to people, cars, boats, planes, opinions etc. You could say for example, that 10% of people sampled in an opinion poll thought the government were doing a good job. The sample sizes would be large so 10% might well be 1000 people out of a sample of 10,000 individuals. In reality, it would be more like 1159 out of 11,590 persons sampled.

Percentiles (sometimes abbreviated to 'centiles') give you an idea of the relative standing or ranking of a particular value within a certain group, such as belonging to the upper third or the lower fifth of a class at school. They are used extensively for comparison of examinations results. Imagine you have a school class of 20 pupils and your daughter was fourth from top in a recent test. You could say she finished in the top 20%. That is equivalent to 80/100 and is termed 'above the 80th percentile'. Conversely, if someone else's child did badly and finished fourth from bottom (16th) that equates to 20/100 and the 20th percentile. The number of exam entrants might change but your offspring could still be at the 80th percentile if they were, say, 10th from top in a class of 50 entrants.

- If you know the difference between percentages and percentiles and wish to demonstrate your intellectual superiority, use percentiles ruthlessly. If you wish to be really unkind, do not use an explanatory adjective like 'very well' or 'badly' for example, 'my son did very well and finished right at the 80th percentile'. Instead, say 'my son finished at the 80th centile' and keep a dead straight face!

Also, it may be useful to introduce the term 'decile' – or basically dividing the group into tenths! If there are 80 pupils in a class, then the decile is 8 pupils i.e. one tenth of the total number. You might twist the dagger further in your opponent by adding 'there was no-one else anywhere near my daughter's decile'.

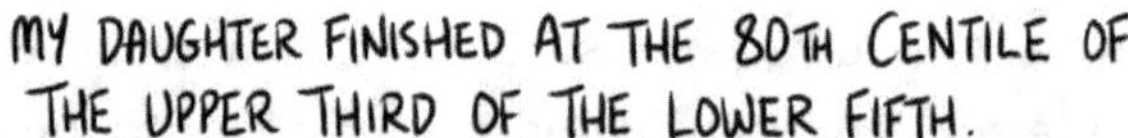

Cartoon 5.5

HOW TO DECEIVE WITH STATISTICS

As discussed above, bias may be inadvertent or a deliberate form of misleading or cheating. Here are some other techniques that are employed in debate and especially by advertisers.

1. **Use the term 'Average' to indicate either the Mean, Mode or Median** – whichever suits your purpose best. Look at Figure 5.3. The data are not distributed Normally, they are skewed to the right i.e. towards the higher incomes with the longer 'tail'. The graph represents the number of people (on the vertical axis, ordinate, or y axis!) plotted against gross income (on the horizontal axis, abscissa or X axis). Imagine you live in a rich suburb and wish to argue that incomes are not that high. You could say 'the average family income in my suburb is quite modest' referring to the Mode – which is an incorrect use of the term 'Average'. Your opponent might respond:

'I totally disagree. If you take the <u>Mean</u> and define the average correctly as the sum of their incomes divided by the number of people, then the average family in your area are, in fact, quite high earners'.

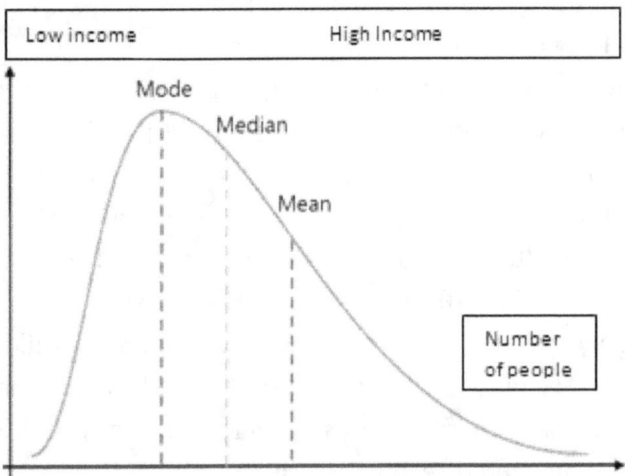

Figure 5.3. A graph skewed to the right to show number of people plotted against income.

Whenever someone uses the term 'average', <u>always challenge it</u> and ask whether they are referring to normal or skewed data and whether they are talking about the mode, median or mean and ask for at least the mean and median values, because large discrepancies between the two tell you about differences in the population. For some reason the term 'median' has become popular substituted term amongst politicians and you can now guess the likely reasons for this.

2. **Quote outliers.** All investigations have extreme values. There will always be some people in the third standard deviation area (see figure 5.1). You could mischievously state that you know of people who have extremely low incomes in your locality, without mentioning that they are exceptional and account for a very small part of the overall picture (see Figure 5.3). Similarly for high earners. Differences between the mean and median can tell you where extreme values may lie.

3. **Use relative rather than absolute percentages**. This is a wicked ploy of politicians, the media, zealots, and big Pharma alike. Here is an example:
   - If 10 out of 100 people claim some form of social benefit and the number of claimants increases to 12 in 100 this is a *relative* increase of 20% (12/100 –divided by 10/100 = 12/10 or 1.2, 20% more) but an *absolute* increase of only 2% (12/100-10/100 = 2/100). The denominator is the bottom figure, here either 10 or 100. Thus, it is essential to specify which denominator is applied. The wily proponent is likely to quote a 20% increase, to reinforce their view that people claiming social benefit are all scroungers and they are on the increase. You should respond by saying:

     'Do you mean an absolute or relative increase of the number of claimants? What denominator are you using?'

Hopefully, the respondent does not know the difference between the two measures and even more likely will be unable to quote both sets of data. In media interviews, such percentages *hardly ever* get challenged and the vast majority of data cited are *relative values*.

A similar strategy is used by Big Pharma (and even by apparently impartial doctors) when comparing a new with old treatment. For example, it is correct practice to compare a new therapy for multiple sclerosis with an older well-established one. A key measurement is the number of disease relapses after introduction of the new treatment compared to traditional treatment. The correct approach is to examine the *absolute* reduction of relapse number, but many prefer the *relative* metric because the results are nearly always far more impressive – and of course these help sales.

4. **Omit the Denominator.** This approach, which is basically an extension of the above, is used repeatedly and mischievously by many politicians, yet once more, they are virtually never opposed.

Prior to elections, campaigners may try to humiliate the opposing side by phrases such as:

'Knife crime up 60%'; 'Robbery up 86%'; 'Council tax up 10%' etc. These statements have _no meaning whatsoever_ as they all lack clarity on the denominator.

'Apple computers are far more reliable than Microsoft'. This may well be true but there are far more Microsoft based computers (about 70% of the world market) than Apple, so the number of faulty machines that come to light is likely to be higher with Microsoft. Without a denominator no judgement can be made.

Another example. Say there was an outbreak of measles in one County, with 30 new cases and two deaths, whereas the year before there were just 14 cases and no fatalities. This might be used to support a proposal for more funding of social services etc. At face value, this is more than a doubling of the number of cases. You should ask what was the denominator – in other words what was the population of vulnerable children, so it could be established how many were at risk of measles? You might also enquire how many cases were detected in a nearby county of similar population where social services were better. Without the denominator you cannot put information into perspective. You should always compare 'like with like'. Furthermore. without a denominator you have no idea of the margin of error as explained above. In essence, there should be statistical analysis to determine whether the apparent outbreak could have occurred by chance alone. This would require evaluation of data going back several years to assess fluctuations.

This point is so vital that I make no apology for yet another example:

> In April 2021, the UK recorded a total of 4,367,291 cases of Covid-19 compared to Belgium who logged only 993,613 instances. A first sight this suggests a much worse situation in the UK, which it is, if you consider the whole nation *but it is not* when adjusted for population size! There are about 68.2 million people in UK and just 11.6 million in Belgium. When the figures are adjusted for the denominator i.e. number of cases per million people, Belgium is in fact *worse* off with 78,104/million cases compared to 64,075/million cases for the UK (assuming a small margin of error!).

5. **Juggle the length of the vertical or horizontal axis.** There are multiple ways of changing the presentation of data on graphs, to make them suit a particular viewpoint. Here are some examples:

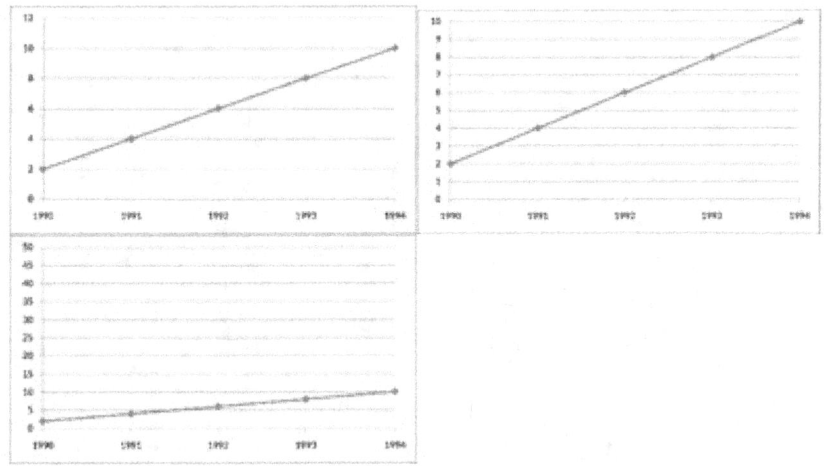

Figure 5.4. The original graph is on the left and the raw data are identical in all three. The horizontal axis shows 'Years' and has not been changed in any of the three figures. The central graph shows a slightly steeper slope, achieved by leaving off the original maximum value of 12 on the vertical axis. Such redrawing could be used to show better sales growth for example. In the right-hand graph, the vertical axis has been extended from 12 to 50 thus giving the impression of a more gradual change. A similar deception can be made by doubling the height or width of the graph dimensions.

Reproduced from: Smallman12q - Own work, CC0, https://commons.wikimedia.org/w/index.php?curid=20398310.

In a similar vein, the vertical axis of a bar chart can be altered, as in figure 5.5.

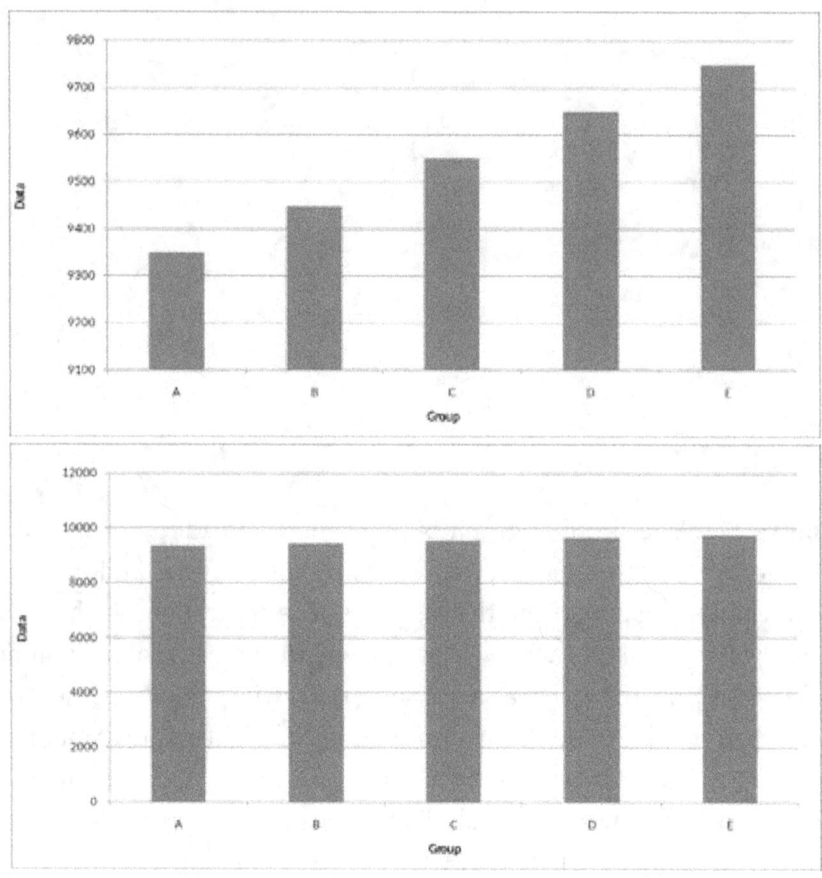

Figure 5.5. Both bar charts display exactly the same raw data, but the vertical axis is elongated in the right figure. If you wish to show change the left chart would be appropriate. If you want to show stability, select the one on the right! Reproduced from Smallman12q - Own work, CC0, https://commons.wikimedia.org/w/index.php?curid=20059376

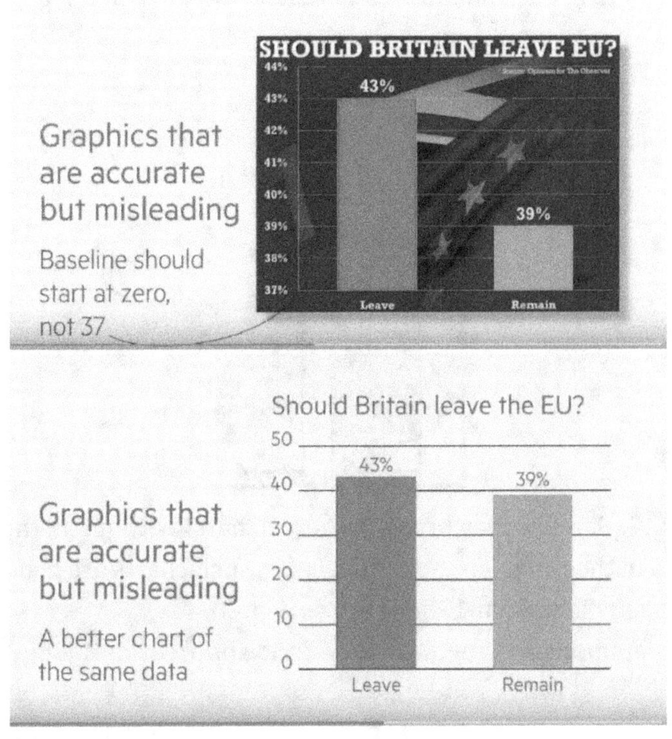

Figure 5.6. An example of truncating the vertical axis values (top figure, at 37%) to convey the false impression of a large difference in support for leaving the EU. Note, there are no error bars to reflect the accuracy and size of the sample (margin of error). There should also be tests to determine whether the percentages differ significantly from each other. In essence the top chart is meaningless, but very likely to deceive the public. Reproduced from Vasyl 10 - Own work, CC BY-SA 4.0, https://commons.wikimedia.org/w/index.php?curid=80137579

Another similar manipulation is to display a bar with a zig-zag as in Figure 5.7

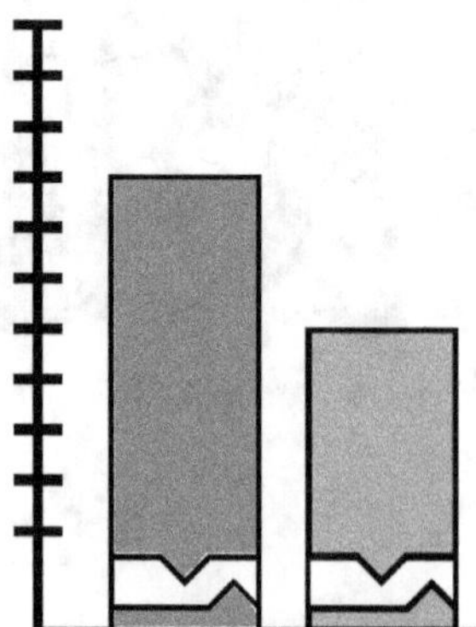

Figure 5.7. This shows a break in the two bars. Without all the numbers in the range on the vertical axis, such charts are generally worthless. By Smallman12q - Own work, CC0, https://commons.wikimedia.org/w/index.php?curid=20387734

LUCK, CHANCE AND PROBABILITY ISSUES

When a sportsman appears to be on a 'winning streak' it is often attributed to good luck. More often, the reality is that the player practises intensively. Tiger Woods, the golfer, encapsulated the term 'luck' perfectly, with the statement:

'The more I practice, the luckier I get'.

Luck, both good and bad is entertaining mythology but from the scientists' perspective, entirely nonsensical, cluttered with head-on conflicts and cultural idiosyncrasies. Regularly we wish someone 'good luck' or if a prize is won in a lottery for example, we call that 'good luck' or say, 'lucky you'. Some people are apparently endowed with good fortune in gambling, sport, lotteries etc. They are encouraged by *selective recall bias* to remember and brag about chance occasions where they were lucky and the linked fallacy, *'post hoc ergo propter hoc'* (after this therefore because of this). Remember, a*ssociation does not indicate causation'*. Virtually no-one brags about or even mentions their losses in gambling etc.

There are depressing facts about individuals who invest in the stock market through a broker. Around 90-95% of clients return a loss at the end of their accounting year (Barber et al 2008; Beckman 1983).

'Playing the lottery is a tax on people who are bad at maths'

Cartoon 5.6

Have you ever visited Las Vegas? You will be inundated with advertisements saying '95% pay-outs guaranteed' or more. How could you possibly lose? You give them $100 and get back $95? Is that winning?? Say the pay-out is 95% and you wager two credits

($2) per spin on a slot machine. For every $2 spin, you will lose 5% of that bet or 10 cents. If you limit your spend to $10, it will take on average about 50 spins before your credit is less than $1 and you can play no more. If you are 'lucky' you might win a small amount or even the Jackpot. So, what are your chances of winning the Jackpot? If you are playing a typical 3-reel slot machine with 20 symbols on each reel, the odds of hitting a single scoring symbol is 1:19. To hit all three symbols the probability is 1 in 20x20x20 or 1:8,000. Who wants to play when the chances of winning are this bad? Only those oblivious to reality? Some machines appear to deliver seductive winning streaks but on modern computer operated machines, every spin generates a random number *that has nothing to do with* previous numbers. If you have won something, then cash out before it's too late! The only people who have 'luck' are the owners of the casino. If they did not, they would be bankrupt in no time. Worse still are national lotteries. For example, the odds of a jackpot win in the EuroMillions lottery are 1:139 million! Despite all the discouraging maths, millions of people gamble every week in lotteries and some people do win! Random events happen in a gambler's favour and presumably that is what is meant by 'luck'? Conversely, if there were no winners despite extremely long odds, any lottery would go out of business quickly – so are winners 'created' by devious managers? Also remember the old saying 'for every winner there is a loser'. In other words, the winner is in a sense, capitalising on the misfortune and loss of others; an interesting moral debate!

Gambler's fallacy. This is the widespread tendency to assume that <u>previous</u> results of *known random events* like tossing a coin or rolling dice will influence <u>future</u> events. In roulette for example, the unsophisticated gambler will predict that if there are several black numbers in sequence then the chances of a subsequent red number are high. Although there are scores of anecdotes in support, *this is scientific rubbish*. At the Monte Carlo casino in 1913, the ball fell on black 26 times in a row. The statistical chances of this happening randomly are about 66 million to 1. Despite this, the odds of a black at the 27th spin still remain 50:50, ignoring the green zero or double zero and assuming that the wheel was not compromised illegally. To repeat: previous results of random events *do not and cannot* affect future events. When flipping a coin, the prospects of heads or tails are equal, always assuming that the coin has not been tampered with. When rolling dice, the chances of a 6, are 1:6. In both examples there may a string of heads or a run of sixes, but if the coin is flipped or the dice rolled several hundred times the chances of heads versus tails remain at 1:2 or 1:6 for dice.

Casinos make their money because of this property and the human tendency to behave as if previous random events influence the future. In roulette, the house pays 35 to 1 for a bet on a particular number. In Europe there are 37 numbers on the board whereas in USA there is a double zero in USA, making 38. The casino wins with a 0 or 00 since those betting either red or black lose, a guaranteed profit against the red and black betters. The House pays out 35 to 1 for a bet on any particular number giving on average, 2 or 3 chances out of 37 or 38 to beat anyone who put specific money on any one number. Thus, the casino doesn't care how one bets in roulette because there is no strategy that will, in the long run, take away their guaranteed profit – they have no need to cheat.

Luck and chance come up regularly in debates and many people seem to cling to the possibility of some supernatural power that works against cruel mathematical probabilities. A useful word in this context is 'stochastic': it just means 'random', but only a few people will have heard of it. Use it remorselessly! Follow this with the gambler's fallacy and you should win the debate easily – without need for any luck to be on your side!

I DON'T CARE WHAT THOSE UNIVERSITY TYPES SAY- I'M ON A WINNING STREAK- LOOK, 4 REDS IN A ROW! A BLACK IS BOUND TO COME UP NEXT!

Cartoon 5.7

CHAPTER 6

LOW FREQUENCY WORDS AND PHRASES

Normally a dictionary is placed at the back of the book. That guarantees it will never be read, so I make no apology for listing low frequency words here, livened up by some cartoons! Knowledge of uncommon words or phrases has the potential to embarrass your opponent, who may feel uncomfortable to ask for a definition or may have lost the thread in the debate. Here are some favourite words and phrases used by the media and debaters. The definition is deliberately kept short and restricted to their commoner uses. I suggest you read through the list quickly to begin with and then re-read until you have learnt them all.

A

- Ablate. To remove or damage tissue. Usually in a surgical context.
- Ableism. Discrimination in favour of able-bodied people
- Abrogate. Do away with. Synonyms: repeal, revoke, repudiate, rescind
- Acerbic. An unpleasant spoken or written comment. This may be witty, sarcastic or ironic
- Acolyte. An assistant. Originally it referred the clergy but now it is applied to any helper
- Acme. The point at which something is at its best. Similar to zenith or apogee. The opposite (antonym) is 'Nadir'
- Acronym. An abbreviation formed by the first letters of words. NATO stands for North Atlantic Treaty Organisation. SCUBA stands for 'Self Contained Underwater Breathing Apparatus'

- Acquit. To be found not guilty at a trial
- Ad hoc. As or when needed
- Ad nauseam. Annoying repetition of a fact or statement
- Aggrandisement. To increase the power or importance of something or somebody. Self-aggrandisement is an attempt to make oneself appear more important
- Aggregate. A majority view or combination of items
- Algorithm. Poorly defined, but usually applied to a set of instructions, typically in a computer programme
- Alliteration. Use of the same consonant at the beginning of successive words. For example: 'Round the rugged rocks the ragged rascal ran"
- Allegory. Usually, a story or play that delivers a particular message
- Allure. Powerful attraction
- Allusive. Referring to something indirectly. Allude is the associated verb
- Anarchy. Lawlessness
- Animosity. A strong feeling of hatred or hostility. Similar to enmity
- Anodyne: inoffensive. In medicine: a painkiller
- Antonym. A word meaning the opposite
- Anachronism. Out of date. Old fashioned
- Anthropocentric. The assumption that humans are the most important entity in the universe. It is often associated with the belief that animals and insects etc. are a less worthy species. 'Anthropocentric vanity' is a good phrase, implying a pompous belief in the superiority and importance of humans over animals
- Antithesis. Opposite idea
- Antipathy. Strong feeling of dislike
- Aperçu. An outline or good point. Often used in the plural – apercus
- Apperceive. To have consciousness of oneself. 'Agency' is a related noun
- Apocryphal. Legendary

- Apogee. The highest point in development of something. In astronomy it refers to the point in orbit that is furthest from Earth e.g. of the Moon, a satellite or spaceship
- Apotheosis. The perfect form of something. Elevation to divine status
- Apposite. Appropriate
- Appropriation. Taking something for your own use usually without permission
- Archetype. Something very typical. Usually applied to a typical person or behaviour
- Archipelago. A group of islands.
- Artisan. Skilled worker
- Assuage. To lessen a concern or to satisfy a desire
- Astroturfing. Organisations funded by large corporations who pretend to represent grassroot opinion i.e. that of the man in the street
- Atone. To make amends for a wrongdoing
- Augur. To foretell
- Autonomous: automatic. Medically, the autonomic nervous system controls responses such as fight or flight and basic digestive functions
- Avignon presidency. This concerned Donald Trump, who tried to continue governing when he refused to accept the result of the 2020 election that he lost to President Joe Biden. It goes back to the Avignon Papacy of the 14th century, in which successive Popes tried to govern from Avignon, rather than Rome.
- Avuncular. A kind and friendly person, usually toward a younger individual

B

- Bacchanalia. A drunken orgy or party
- Badinage. Witty conversation.

- Barter. To exchange one item or service for another without use of money. You might swap a broken old watch for a pint of beer
- Basket case. Something or someone who is useless and unable to cope
- Behemoth. A monster. It is often applied metaphorically to e.g. large corporations.
- Beneficence. Generosity
- Bespoke. Specially made for someone e.g. bespoke tailor or for a specific purpose
- Bête noire. Something or someone that is particularly disliked
- Bedizened. To dress in a very showy or tasteless manner
- Bigamy. The act of marrying someone while already married.
- Bijou. Something small and elegant
- Binary. Similar to dichotomous: yes or no situations

Cartoon 6.1

- Blasé. Casual
- Blind-side. To catch out someone unaware, usually about something unpleasant
- Bling. Ostentatious (showy) jewellery or clothing
- Brobdingnagian. Huge
- Bloviate. To talk at length, particularly in a shallow or pompous manner. Often applied to politicians
- Brougham. A horse-drawn carriage
- Bucolic. Relating to pleasant aspects of the countryside
- Bung. A slang term for a financial bribe
- Burgeoning: flourishing
- Byzantine. An excessively complicated situation or system

C

- Cacophonous. Harsh discordant sounds
- Cahoots. To be in a partnership with someone, usually secretive. 'In cahoots with' is the usual expression
- Caliphate. An Islamic State
- Chameleon. Literally it refers to a particular lizard that can change its skin colour. It often refers to a person whose opinions change according to the situation e.g. a political chameleon
- Camelot. The legendary site of King Author's palace. Often used to describe an idyllic place or period
- Canonical. Typical or classical. In a religious context, it refers to sacred books
- Cantankerous. Bad tempered or argumentative
- Carceral. Relating to prison
- Carte blanche. Freedom to do what you want
- Catatonic. Medically this is severe muscular stiffness because of medication side-effects or some types of schizophrenia Informally, it may imply inability to move or think
- Caustic. In science, it refers to a compound that will burn the skin, such as caustic soda (an ingredient of bleach). In

conversation, a caustic remark is something unpleasant or sarcastic

- Cavil. A petty objection. A grouse. A caviller is someone who grumbles repeatedly
- Chagrin. Something annoying.
- Chatterati. Non-complementary reference to people who talk a lot – usually trivia.
- Chimera. A mythical animal made up of parts from different animals. In Greek mythology it is a monster with a lion's head, goat's body, and a serpent's tail. Sometimes the word is used to convey an illusion. In biology, it refers to cells with two differing sets of DNA. Thus, a human cell may possess a mixture of male and female chromosomes, namely XY and XX.
- Chumocracy. A ruling elite comprising people who went to the same schools or universities. It is a portmanteau word (see below) combining 'Chum' with 'ocracy' that relates to various types of government (democracy, autocracy etc.)

Cartoon 6.2

- Chutzpah. Extreme self-confidence. Similar meaning to hubris
- Clandestine. Something done secretly – usually illegally
- Codify. To convert laws or diseases etc. into a set of codes
- Coerce. To force someone to undertake an action or to say something they do not wish to
- Cogito ergo sum. I think, therefore I am. Attributed to Descartes, the philosopher
- Colloquial. Informal everyday language. Similar to vernacular.
- Commission. There are several meanings but the one that occurs often in conversation, is 'sin of commission' which means something immoral that you did, compared to 'sin of omission' which is something you should have done.

Cartoon 6.3

- Concision. Brevity
- Conclave. A private or secret meeting. Originally the term referred to a meeting of catholic cardinals to elect a new pope
- Concomitant. Accompanying

- Conducive. Causing or producing something
- Confiscate. To seize property or belongings
- Conflate. Combine
- Consigliere. Member of a Mafia family who acts as an adviser
- Consignor. The buyer of goods
- Corollary. A usually inevitable consequence
- Coterie. A small select group of people
- Craven. Cowardly, lacking courage. Often applied in a contemptuous manner
- Cui bono. Who stands to gain?
- Curmudgeonly. Bad tempered
- Curry favour. Use of flattery to gain support or some other advantage

D

- Decorum. Behaviour that is in good taste
- De facto. In fact
- Defamation. The act of damaging the reputation of someone by slander or libel
- Demagogue. A political leader who tries to raise support by appealing to prejudice rather than reason. A rabble-rouser or soap-box orator
- Demean. To lower respect for someone. It may also refer to a task which is not dignified
- Demeanour. Outward behaviour
- Demure. Modest or shy
- Denizen. Usually applied to a person (or animal) who lives in a particular place, such as a forest. Also applied to a regular inhabitant of a night club or bar
- Denigrate. To belittle someone or something. Similar to disparage or humiliate
- De Rigueur. Something demanded by fashion, such as a particular hair style

- Destitute. Penniless
- Diaspora. Usually refers to the migration of any population from their original homeland
- Diatribe. Bitter verbal attack
- Dichotomous or dichotomy. A 'yes' or 'no' circumstance or situation where there are just two opposing options. Similar to binary
- Dirigiste. Strong economic planning by government
- Disambiguate. To clarify a text
- Discombobulate. To confuse
- Disenfranchised. Not having the right to vote or having some other right removed
- Disparaging. To belittle something or someone
- Divest. Remove or deprive something such as power or money
- Doppelganger. An apparition or double of a living person
- Double entendre. A word or phrase with two meanings
- Dork. Slang for a stupid or awkward person
- Dystopian. An imaginary society that has descended into barbarism

E

- Ebullient. Cheerful; full of energy
- Echelon. A particular level of authority. A common phrase is 'the higher echelons of power'
- Eclectic. Use of multiple sources of knowledge or styles
- Effete. Weak and powerless
- Egregious. Conspicuously bad
- Emasculate. To weaken
- Empirical. Based on experience rather than theory
- Emulate. To copy the achievements of someone else
- Enmity. A feeling of hate or hostility. Similar meaning to animosity or antipathy
- Ensconce. To settle in a safe, comfortable place

- Ephemeral. Short-lived
- Epigrammatic. A short witty comment.
- Epiphany. Sudden major realisation of e.g. the truth, or solution of a problem. Eureka moment
- Equanimity. Calmness
- Equipoise. Something that is in balance. In science it refers to opposing theories which are supported equally
- Epistemology. The theory of knowledge
- Erudition. Having great knowledge
- Ersatz. An imitation or fake product
- Espouse. To support something, typically an idea or action
- Et tu Brutus? Meaning 'Even you Brutus?'. Sometimes abbreviated to just 'et tu'. This refers to Julius Caesar's last words in Shakespeare's play. Julius Caesar, when he discovers the infidelity of his friend, Brutus.
- Euphemism. A mild way of expressing something unpleasant. 'Sadly, he passed on' for death
- Exacerbate. Aggravate
- Exigent. Requiring immediate attention. Urgent
- Exonerate. To clear blame from someone
- Expiation. Making amends for guilt or wrongdoing
- Exponential. Although it does have a precise mathematical definition, in lay conversation, it usually means phenomenally rapid growth – of infection or money etc.
- Extirpate. To eradicate or destroy completely
- Extrapolate. Extend a method or conclusion. Often applied to curves in graphs to predict a future value
- Extrinsic. External. In medicine it refers to parts that are outside the main organs, such as the extrinsic eye muscles. See opposite word, intrinsic.

Cartoon 6.4

F

- Factitious. Invented
- Factotum. A person who has several jobs and responsibilities
- Farrago. A confused mixture
- Faustian pact: an agreement with the Devil whereby the legendary Faust exchanges his soul for unlimited knowledge and worldly pleasures
- Feral. Wild. May apply to humans or animals
- Fifth column. A group or individual who support enemies of their country in secret. Similar meaning to a double-agent
- Filibuster. To prolong a debate deliberately (usually in parliament), to prevent a motion or bill being passed
- Folie à Deux. A delusion shared by two people. Where three people are involved, it is a Folie à trois
- Forswear. Agree to give up something or do without
- Freeloader. A person that takes advantage of someone else's generosity but gives nothing in return
- Fubar. Slang for damaged beyond all repair

- Fugazi. Slang for something that is fake or severely damaged
- Furlough: leave of absence from work
- Frisson: sudden strong feeling of excitement or fear

G

- Galling. Something annoying
- Garrulous. Talkative. Same meaning as 'loquacious'.
- Genome. A collection of genes.
- Genre. A particular style in music, art or literature
- Genuflect. To bend a knee as a token of respect.
- Gerrymander. To manipulate electoral boundaries to favour one particular political party.
- Gestalt. An overall impression
- Glean. To gather information

H

- Hagiography. A biography that displays undue reverence
- Harangue. To speak to someone in an aggressive manner
- Hegemony. Political or cultural dominance
- Heuristics. The process of discovery by one's own experience
- Homophobia. Prejudice toward homosexual people
- Hubris. Over-confident behaviour. The 'hubris syndrome' allegedly affected Margaret Thatcher and Tony Blair and many dictators. Hubris often forebodes a major downfall
- Hustings. A political meeting
- Hybrid. Something that has two different components. For example, a hybrid car could have both petrol and electric engines
- Hyperbole. An exaggerated claim or statement
- Hypochondriac. Someone overly concerned about their health. Same meaning as valetudinarian
- Hypocrite. Someone who pretends to have beliefs or feelings they do not

- Hypothecate. In politics: to allocate the income raised by a tax for a specific purpose. Similar to ring-fencing. It also means to pledge an asset in place of a debt, as in securing a mortgage on your house
- Hyperbole. Exaggeration.

I

- Idiosyncratic. A strange way of behaving or thinking. A quirk
- Immolate: kill or offer as a sacrifice, especially by burning.
- Impecunious. Having little money
- Imposter syndrome. Having doubts about one's own skills and achievements. Self-doubt
- Impugn. To challenge
- Inane. Something very stupid. Usually applied to unwanted remarks
- Incandescent. Fuming with emotion – usually anger
- Incendiary. Tending to stir up conflict
- Incorrigible. Not capable of reform. An incorrigible liar.
- Incumbent. Noun: the person who holds a particular job. Adjective: an obligation to undertake a particular task.
- Inflected. Usually means to be influenced by something or someone
- Innocuous. Harmless
- Inundate. To be overwhelmed
- Insouciance. Casual lack of concern
- Intransigent. Unwilling to change one's views

Cartoon 6.5

- Intifada. Arabic word for a rebellion
- Inclement. Unpleasant – usually applied to weather
- Internecine. Warfare where both sides suffer. Struggles between members of the same country. In politics it refers to bitter fights within the same political group
- Intrinsic. Something particularly important or essential. In medicine it applies to internal body parts. See opposite word; extrinsic
- Invidious. Likely to cause anger or distress in someone.
- Irascible. Bad tempered
- Iterative. Repetitive action
- Isthmus. A narrow strip of land with water on either side
- Inveterate. Habitual. For example, an inveterate liar is someone who continually lies

Cartoon 6.6

J

- Jape. A joke. Japery is to act like a clown
- Juxtaposed. Next to. Places, objects or people who are alongside

K

- Kitsch. Something tasteless – usually applied to art

L

- Languorous. Idle pleasure
- Lascivious. Lustful
- Libel. Unpleasant *written* remarks about someone. Note that slander refers to unpleasant *spoken* comments
- Libertine. A person (usually male) who has sexual relations with many women. Also applies to someone who is freethinking – so use with care!
- Loquacious. Talkative, garrulous

- Lorgnette. A pair of glasses, held in front of the eyes by a long handle
- Lothario. A man whose chief interest is in seducing women. A rake, playboy and libertine have similar meanings

- Machiavellian. Use of cunning behaviour. It refers to the Italian philosopher Niccolo Machiavelli who wrote the book: 'The Prince' that encourages behaviour whereby 'the end justifies the means'
- Maelstrom. A whirlpool
- Magnanimous. Generous
- Malfeasance. Dishonest or illegal behaviour usually in reference to a business or someone in high authority
- Manacle. A handcuff
- Mansplaining. Explaining something by a male to a female in condescending fashion
- Mantra. Statement or slogan that is repeated often. Usually in a political context
- Masochism. Taking pleasure in hurting oneself. Opposite is sadism, where there is pleasure in hurting others
- Maraud. To raid and plunder, usually in the context of war
- Mea culpa. Through my fault
- Meme. An idea or behaviour that is passed on from one person to another by imitation or social media
- Ménage à trois. A domestic arrangement in which a married couple and the lover of one of them live together
- Mendicant. A beggar or scrounger
- Mercenary. Noun: an unofficial soldier. Adjective: someone only interested in money
- Metaverse. A computer-generated virtual reality space allowing users to interact
- Miasma. Poisonous fumes or pollutants. Dangerous emissions from dead bodies

- Minion. A follower, usually a servant (or similar) of an important person
- Miniscule. An exceedingly small amount. Minutiae has similar meaning
- Miscreant. A person who has done something wrong or unlawful
- Misogyny. Prejudice against females
- Mitigate. To make something less severe. Mitigating circumstances may reduce the length of a criminal's prison sentence
- Mitzvah. A commandment
- Modicum. Small amount. A modicum of decorum means a small amount of good manners or taste

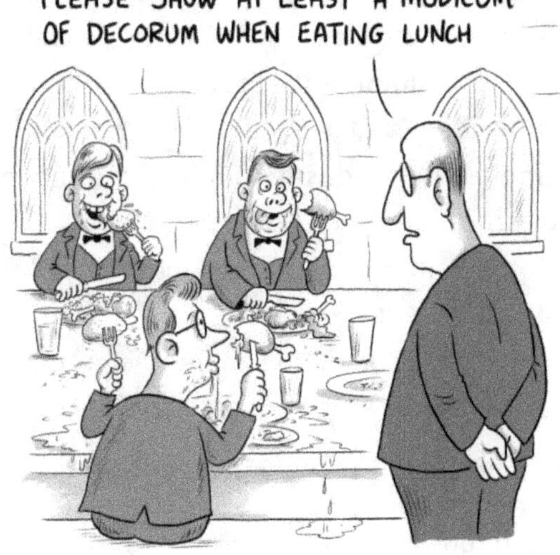

Cartoon 6.7

- Modus operandi. A particular method of doing something
- Mojo. Magical charm
- Monarchy. Government with a king or queen at its head
- Moratorium. A temporary suspension of an activity, such as a loan
- Mordant. Biting humour
- Motley fool. A clown or idiot
- Mundane. Dull or boring

- Nadir. Lowest or worst point. Opposite is acme or zenith.
- Narcissism. Self-love
- Necromancer. Someone who claims to communicate with deceased people and predict the future. Similar to a spiritualist
- Nefarious. Wicked
- Neologism. A newly invented word
- Nepotism. Unfair use of power to give important jobs to family members
- Noetic. Intellectual ability
- Non sequitur. An illogical conclusion
- Nostradamus. A 16th century physician who made several apparently correct predictions about world events, including the Great Fire of London, the French Revolution, the rise of Napoleon and Hitler and many more
- Nostrum. Ineffective medicine sold by a charlatan. Or: a dubious remedy to bring about social reform
- Nuance. Noun: minor difference. Adjective is 'nuanced' which means subtly different
- Nugate. To trivialise something and not focus on the real issues

O

- Obdurate. Stubborn
- Obsequious. Cringing or sycophantic. Excessively obedient
- Oleaginous. Literally means 'oily'. Often refers to someone who is too friendly or insincere
- Oligarchy. Government by a small group of people
- Omerta. A code of silence about criminal activity and a refusal to give evidence to the police. It is practiced widely by the Mafia
- Onomatopoeia. A word that resembles the sound that it describes e.g. hissing, rustle, beep
- Opprobrium. Harsh criticism

- Ornery. Irritable disposition
- Ossuary. A container or room for the bones of the dead
- Ostentatious. Pretentious. Usually applied to showy clothing, jewellery or property
- Ostracise. To exclude someone from society or a group
- Oxymoron. A contradictory phrase e.g., deafening silence; an open secret

P

- Panacea. A cure for everything
- Pantheon. A temple containing graves of Gods or famous people
- Patriarchy. A social system governed by men
- Paragon. A perfect example of something or someone e.g., paragon of virtue
- Paramour. A lover, particularly an illicit or secret lover
- Paraphernalia. Any collection of equipment to aid a sport or employment. For example, the contents of a sports bag or tool box
- Pariah. An individual who is despised – a social pariah. Also applies to an outcast state such as Myanmar (Burma), Syria or Afghanistan where human rights are not respected
- Pari passu. At the same rate or time. Note: *in tandem* means one after the other
- Parlance. A particular way of speaking
- Parsimonious. Miserly. In statistics: the simplest explanation
- Partisan. Staunch supporter of a political party
- Passé. Out of date
- Patrician. An aristocrat or nobleman
- Peccadillo. A minor fault
- Pedagogue. A teacher, usually strict
- Penchant. A strong liking for something or a particular action
- Penury. Severe poverty
- Peon. An unskilled worker doing menial work, sometimes to pay off a debt

- Per se. In itself

- Perfect storm. A combination of unfavourable events leading to disaster. Often applied to economics to predict a stock market crash. Similar to the phrase 'a recipe for disaster'

- Perfunctory. Something done without real interest or feeling. A perfunctory smile or handshake

- Perjury. Deliberate lying in a court of law

- Peroration. The summary of a speech. Sometimes used to describe a long boring speech

- Pertinent. Relevant

- Pervasive. Something that is widespread and usually unwelcome. For example: corruption or ageism

- Philanderer. A womaniser. Similar to Lothario, rake or libertine

- Phlegmatic: Unemotional. Sanguine is the opposite, meaning optimistic

- Pique. A feeling of resentment resulting from an offence. As a verb it means to arouse interest

- Platitude. An overused insincere statement often about morality

- Pogrom. An organised massacre of a particular ethnic group such as the German Jews by Hitler. Similar meaning to genocide

- Polemic. An aggressive attack on the opinions or principles of another person

- Politburo. The main decision-making committee of a communist party

- Polymath. Someone who is well read and knowledgeable in a wide variety of subjects. Similar to a savant

- Polymorphism. A term used in genetics that refers to normally occurring variants. For example, having blue eyes or brown eyes results from harmless variants in DNA. It usually has little effect on general health

- Portmanteau. Originally it referred to a large leather travelling bag. Now it relates to combined words e.g. 'motel'; a combination of motorist and hotel. 'Podcast' is a combination of 'iPod' and 'broadcast'. 'Brunch' is breakfast and lunch

- Pragmatic. A practical rather than theoretical way of dealing with problems
- Preclude. To prevent from happening
- Predilection. A preference or special liking
- Predicated. Usually means to be based on something like a theory or policy
- Preposterous. Something outrageous
- Prerequisite. A prior condition
- Prerogative. A right or privilege for a particular individual or class e.g., the Queen
- Presage. Foretell something. Similar meaning to augur
- Prescient. Predicting future events correctly. Having great foresight
- Preternatural. Out of the ordinary
- Prevaricate. To avoid answering a question directly, often by lying
- Pro bono. Something done for free. Especially in a legal context
- Procrastinate. Delay
- Profligate. Wasteful
- Proleptic. Anticipating. A proleptic appointment is a temporary position that assumes a permanent job will be made later
- Prorogue: adjournment of parliament
- Prosaic. Literally, it means having the style of prose instead of poetry. Metaphorically it applies to something lacking imagination. Mundane
- Proselyte. Someone who converts from one opinion, religion or political party to another
- Provenance. History of ownership, usually relating to a valuable work of art or literature
- Proxy. On behalf of. Murder by proxy is killing someone by acting on orders of another
- Psephology. The science of political elections and voting trends
- Pseudonymise. Storage of personal data by use of numbers and letters that can only be accessed by use of a key. It is slightly less secure than completely anonymous data

- Punitive. Punishing. A punitive amount of work or tax demand
- Purdah. The Islamic practice of a) covering up a woman's body with long clothing and a facial scarf b) using screens at home to prevent visitors seeing women therein. Also applied to the period between announcement of an election date and the election day itself
- Pusillanimous. Cowardly or lacking interest
- Putsch. A violent attempt to overthrow a government. A coup
- Pyrrhic victory. A successful battle/court case etc. that leaves the winner worse off

Cartoon 6.8

Q

- Quintessential. Something that is perfect
- Quid pro quo. One favour for another
- Quixotic. Extremely idealistic. Unrealistic or impractical suggestions. See Tilting at Windmills

- Raconteur. A storyteller
- Rambunctious. Unrestrained or boisterous
- Realpolitik. A political system based on practical rather than ideological principles
- Recidivism. The tendency of a convicted criminal to reoffend
- Recombinant. A term applied to genetic manipulation whereby DNA or RNA from one species (typically a virus or bacterium) is joined to the DNA/RNA of another
- Reconcile. To restore friendly relations e.g., 'their differences were reconciled.' In finance, to make accounts consistent with each other
- Redoubt. Noun: a safe place, usually in warfare. Adjective: impressive. For example, 'a redoubtable debater'
- Rendition. A performance, typically of a play or opera. It also refers to the practice of sending suspected terrorists to another country for interrogation by torture
- Repartee. Quick and witty style of conversation
- Rescind: cancel
- Resiled. To abandon a course of action
- Redact. To edit
- Redolent. Reminiscent of
- Replete. Full, especially when referring to meals
- Repugnant. Something that is extremely distasteful. Abhorrent or disgusting
- Riven. Split apart
- Roil. Literally, it means stirring a liquid to disturb its sediment. Metaphorically – to annoy or stir up trouble
- Rubric. A formal set of instructions. Also means a category
- Rumbustious. Unruly. Often applied to football fans

- Sadism. Taking pleasure in hurting others
- Salient. Prominent
- Savant. Someone with exceptional knowledge or ability
- Salubrious. Promoting good health or wealth
- Sanguine. Optimistic. Phlegmatic is the opposite
- Sangfroid. The ability to stay calm when under pressure
- Sapphist. A Lesbian
- Scabrous. Literally means covered with scabs. Metaphorically, it infers something indecent or shocking
- Scatological. Referring to faeces often in a humorous manner
- Schism. A division between strongly opposed parties – particularly church leaders and politicians
- Schmaltz. Excessively sentimental
- Schtum. Silent
- Schlock. Cheap goods or material. Trash or bling
- Scintilla. A very small amount
- Scion. Descendant of a wealthy family

Cartoon 6.9

- Scrupulous. Having moral integrity. The opposite is used more often: unscrupulous
- Scurrilous. Making scandalous claims about someone's reputation
- Secular. Having no particular religious view
- Secession. Noun: the act of withdrawal from a formal organisation, political party or State. Secede is the verb
- Sedulous. Showing dedication
- Semantic. The meaning of words. In debate, it is so important to define what is meant by a particular word, especially if it has several meanings
- Sententious. Moralising in a pompous manner
- Sepulchral. Related to a tomb. Gloomy, such as speaking in sepulchral manner
- Sequence (verb). In genetics it means to analyse genes
- Serendipity. By chance
- Sesquipedalian. The habit of using long words
- Seigneurial. To describe someone with great power. Originally a Lord of the Manor
- Schadenfreude: pleasure derived from the misfortune of others
- Sibilance. A figure of speech in which a someone creates a hissing sound, using letter 's' or 'sh'). Often it refers to the high-pitched noise from the wind or sea
- Scintilla. A small trace of something
- Shaman. A person who claims to have access to a spiritual world through a trance-like state. Shamanism refers to the associated religious practice
- Simulacrum. A fake image or copy. Something with superficial likeness
- Skeleton in the cupboard. An unpleasant aspect of someone's past that is best concealed or omitted
- Slander. Voicing disagreeable comments about someone. Slander is *spoken* whereas libel refers to unpleasant *written* statements

- Snowflake (slang). A hypersensitive person
- Solecism. Incorrect use of grammar or bad manners. May mean simply a bad mistake
- Sorority. A female club or fraternity typically at college
- Sobriquet. A nickname
- Sommelier. A wine waiter
- Soupcon. Originally a French word meaning a small amount – usually in the context of cooking

Cartoon 6.10

- Specious. Something that is superficially plausible but wrong
- Spoonerism. An error of speech where the first part of adjacent words are switched. Examples: he went to work by the town drain (down train). You have tasted a whole worm (wasted a whole term); poopin' on Snutin (snooping on Putin)
- Stalking horse. In politics, it is a devious manoeuvre whereby a candidate is put forward to divide the opposition or conceal someone's real candidacy. Similar to parachute or carpet-bagger candidate
- Stridency. Forceful language

- Stochastic. Random
- Sub judice. An ongoing trial that is banned from public discussion
- Sumptuous. Magnificent and expensive. Often applied to dinners e.g., 'a sumptuous banquet'
- Sybaritic. Fondness of pleasure. Similar to Bacchanalia
- Sycophantic. Cringing or obsequious. Excessively obedient
- Sisyphean task. An activity that is endless and futile. The term refers to Sisyphus, a figure of Greek mythology who was given the hopeless task of pushing a boulder uphill repeatedly, only for it to roll back down, every time

Cartoon 6.11

- Sophomore. An American second year college student. Sometimes used to refer to someone with plenty of knowledge but no common sense
- Syllogism. A form of logic based on two premises often with a stupid conclusion. All cats die. Socrates died, therefore Socrates was a cat.

- Take a rain check. A polite way of declining an offer with the implication you might accept later
- Talisman. A lucky charm
- Tautology. Poor writing style with repetition of the same word or phrase. 'His report was reported to be similar to other reports'. 'Personally speaking, I myself believe that...'
- Theocracy. Government by priests
- Thucydides' trap. Often applied to relations between China and USA. It refers to increasing likelihood of war when a super-power, such as China, threatens to displace an established empire such as the USA
- Tilting at windows. Fighting an imaginary enemy. This goes back to the novel by Cervantes (1604) entitled 'Don Quixote' in which a mad knight believed that windmills were giants that needed to be attacked. Highly idealistic behaviour is sometimes called quixotic
- Timeo danaos et dona ferentes. A Latin phrase from Virgil meaning 'I fear the Greeks and gifts they bring'. It is a useful phrase to introduce when someone appears unusually generous but might wish to do harm
- Torquemada. The Spanish inquisitor who was responsible for the deaths of thousands of Jews and alleged witches during the Spanish inquisition
- Triage. Usually applied to emergency medical situations where treatment facilities are limited. A doctor or nurse will triage i.e. separate, casualties in wartime, into a) those who can be treated with a reasonable chance of success and b) those who are relatively well and do not require immediate therapy and others who are beyond help or cannot be resuscitated
- Turf war. A violent dispute between rival groups over disputed territory or business
- Turn King's/Queen's evidence. The practice whereby someone found guilty of a crime offers to supply evidence, such as the

names of other involved criminals, in exchange for lessening
their own sentence
- Turpitude. Highly unacceptable behaviour. Hence the phrase
'moral turpitude.'
- Trope. An idea, phrase, or image

U

- Ubiquitous. Widespread
- Unanimous. Agreed by everyone
- Ultimatum. A final proposal or condition
- Unconscionable. Something unreasonable or unjust
- Underbelly. Metaphorically, an area vulnerable to attack. A
criminal part of society such as a ghetto
- Upping the ante. To increase your demands or risks
- Upset the apple cart. To ruin someone's plans
- Usurp. To gain power by illegal means
- Utilitarian. A practical solution. In philosophy it refers to
measures likely to bring happiness for the greatest number of
people with the lowest prospect of misery

V

- Vade mecum. A brief guide
- Valetudinarian. Someone overly concerned about their health. A
hypochondriac
- Vapid. Uninteresting
- Verbatim. Word for word
- Vernacular. Informal speech or language
- Vespertine. Related to evenings
- Vicarious. A borrowed facility. On behalf of another person
- Vicissitudes. Change of circumstances, usually unpleasant
- Vituperous. Worthy of blame
- Voluptuous. A sexy or curvy female

- Volte face. An abrupt change of thinking. A U-turn

Cartoon 6.12

W

- Woke. Alert to injustice in society, especially racism
- Wonk. An excessively studious person. Similar to nerd or geek

X

- Xenophobia. Dislike of foreigners
- Xenocracy. A government formed by outsiders or foreigners

Y

- Yearling. A racehorse or deer that is one year old
- Yesteryear. Previous
- Yuppie. A fashionable middle-class person with a well-paid job

- Zealous. Enthusiastic.
- Zeitgeist. The defining mood or spirit of a particular generation.
- Zenith: time at which something is most successful. In astronomy it means the highest point reached a planet or the sun.
- Zero sum game. This phrase comes from economics and game theory. It represents the sum of gains and losses by participants which is zero. Poker, chess, and bridge (played for money) are zero sum games because the gains and losses overall, add up to zero.

∞

You should have read all the words in the above list. *Now go back to the start again* and mark the ones you did not know and learn their meaning. Do this repeatedly until you know the lot. Rest assured; it will pay dividends when you have your next debate!

Here are some phrases you might wish to first of all understand and then bring into debate, hoping they will confuse your opponent. Refer back to the list above for the ones you do not know.

- It is really quite antipathetic to try and discombobulate your friend's chagrin with such sequepedalianistic comments. Nothing short of hubristic self-aggrandisement.
- I think our health service is burgeoning with sedulous hypochondriacal valetudinarians. Nothing short of mendicant opportunists who rely on the beneficence of others. Just a load of basket cases without a soupcon of guilt or malaise, buttressed by a succession of anodyne nostrums. (spot the tautologies here!)
- If America wages internecine war with that behemoth of a country, they are facing a task of brobdingnagian proportions.

They should beware the allure of Thucydides' trap and may finish with a Pyrrhic victory if not an outright defeat.

- Our current generation has a never-ending zeitgeist for voluptuous females by lascivious and profligate young men of preposterous moral turpitude. Nothing but specious recidivists who should have been incarcerated at birth!
- Those basket cases should be treated the same as cantankerous toads for expiation.

PART II

THE PRACTICE

Having learnt much theory, now is the time to apply concepts into practice!

Fifteen common debating topics are listed below. The popular arguments for and against are given and strategies you might use to secure a victory or at least an honourable defeat!

None is meant to be a complete debate although the main points for and against are delineated. The mock debates are fundamentally a vehicle for demonstrating how to use some of the strategies given in the first section.

Once more, the points made are invented and do not necessarily reflect the opinions of the author.

Tactical points are italicised in the right hand 'Comments' column.

1. NUCLEAR WEAPONS: SHOULD WE DISARM?

This debate has recurred endlessly since the commencement of the Cold War between the West and USSR/Russia. It was prompted mainly by the development of nuclear weapons by USSR in 1947. The argument is finely balanced but most major Western powers have elected to have nuclear weapons. This debate is between friends Jack and Jill.

Cartoon Pt 2.1

Jack: It's my view that all nuclear weapons in the UK should be got rid of once and for all.

Clear but extreme opening statement.

Jack *avoids answering the point* directly.

Jill: But then we would have no defence against possible enemies like Russia, China, North Korea and maybe Syria or Iran one day.

Jack: Instead, we could improve our conventional forces and invest heavily in the electronic battlefield with robotic soldiers, tanks, drones etc.

Jack again avoids the last statement, at least partially.

Jill: But that would be useless against a nuclear attack.

Jack: We could also invest in better detection of an attack and improving our anti-missile missiles.

He uses the *extreme case* ploy to defend his case.

Jill: Some missiles will always get through. Even one missile could wipe out the whole of London or Birmingham; nothing is really fool-proof at present, you just have to possess nuclear weapons to act as a deterrent.

Jill is backtracking .

Jack: so what's the point of having something that you would never use and if you did, would result in horrendous damage to people on both sides, their housing, health and

Jack *extremes the point* again.

offspring.

Jill: That's the principle of deterrence: both sides would suffer unimaginable losses which they would rather avoid. It's called Mutually Assured Destruction as you know.

She is backtracking.

Jack: That situation is very precarious especially if the nuclear weapons were in the hands of a madman. If that happened on a world-wide scale, there is a danger that human civilization would be wiped out completely.

The *attack with ridicule*. Jack is using ridicule to gain the upper hand.

Jill: I'm talking about a smaller nuclear war with just battlefield nuclear weapons, say within just Europe and Russia

Jill is losing, so her next step is to return to the original subject.

Promotion of cannibalism is a *straw man* attack. Jill never suggested that.

Jack: So it's OK to kill a few million people but not a few billion.

Jill: People could live deep down in caves until the radioactivity settled down.

Jill dodges all counter arguments and skilfully returns to the original question.

Jack: In the UK there are only a few caves that are habitable, and any water would be radioactive assuming you had a Geiger counter to detect it. Apart from that, what about food supplies?

Jack now uses the *emotional approach* – killing with one's own hands. Deliberately uses a *low frequency word* – schadenfreude.

Food and water would be needed for several decades. Are you promoting cannibalism?

Jill: I still maintain that we would be better off with nuclear armaments to scare off anyone who might wish to attack us with such weapons.

Jack: So, if you were Prime Minister and our country was under imminent nuclear attack would you be prepared to press the nuclear button and basically murder millions of innocent foreign civilians as well as promoting infertility and cancers in their offspring? Have you ever killed anyone with your bare hands – a nuclear attack is a thousand times worse. You are advocating the most severe form of schadenfreude.

Jill: I'm not saying what I would do. That is the principle of deterrence: you keep the other side guessing.

Jack hopes that Jill may not have understood the meaning of schadenfreude (pleasure in revenge). Use of such words can upset your opponent if they do not understand them. She dodges the emotional trap and finishes with a stalemate. A form of *constructive ambiguity*.

2. IS TERRORISM JUSTIFIED?

The question of terrorism crops up repeatedly in the media. The usual defence from terrorists is that they are fighting for freedom and the right to self-determination. Bill is interviewing Ben who is not a terrorist but is sympathetic toward them.

Cartoon Pt 2.2

Bill: You don't really believe that anyone, anywhere on this planet can possibly justify terrorism.

Typical *leading question* favoured by interviewers.

Ben: I believe that in certain situations terrorism can be justified. For example, the attacks against the British in East Pakistan in 1971 helped create Bangladesh. Likewise, when the British were forced out of Palestine with the creation of the State of Israel in 1948. Only a few countries now question the rights of these States to exist anymore.

Clear statement of his opinion backed up with facts at the start which is always a good approach. However, the ends do not necessarily justify the means, and this point is overlooked by Bill.

Bill: A doctor friend of mine had his leg blown off in the London bomb attacks of 2005. How can you possibly justify this sort of behaviour in the modern world?

The emotional *anecdote attack* is used here. Useful but weak strategy. This incident is true, actually.

Ben: These are relatively minor acts of terrorism when you compare the 911 attacks in New York that killed over 3000 people in one day. All acts of terrorism are violent and will unfortunately cause death and injury to innocent civilians, but they do seem to work. Some would say the ends justify the means.

He tries to keep the debate calm by using the *passive voice* 'some would say'… although this phrase usually represents the user's own view. *Ends justify the means* is a useful tactical point. It might be useful just to say 'the Machiavellian approach often works' and hope your opponent does not know who was Machiavelli.

Bill: Are you not aware of any

Note the *rhetorical question.* You

peaceful ways of changing society?

Ben: Of course, you can have peaceful protests although they take many years to have effect.

Bill: If everyone adopted terrorism as a means of changing their society, there would be no democracy and whole world would degenerate into a dystopian nightmare.

Ben: I don't think Al Qaeda (ISIS) would share your view. They want to generate fear in the public mind that in turn could result in pressure to change laws and regional boundaries. They are masters of indoctrination especially of young unemployed people with no future and often their raids are carried out with military precision.

Bill: So, what are you saying then – that mass murder is OK if it's carried out with military precision?

Ben: Of course not! The problem with Al Qaeda/ISIS is that their aims (apart from generating fear) are obscure. Do they want Islamic domination of the entire world or their own Caliphate?

should always know the answer to this type of question.

Ben deflects the question on peaceful methods, as that would weaken his case.

Bill is using the '*extreme generalization*' ploy. Also note the use of the *low frequency word* 'dystopia' – meaning a barbaric and chaotic situation without government.

Subtle use of the *passive voice* again, in the first sentence.

Bill is *ridiculing the argument* at the expense of angering his opponent. Also uses the *straw man* ploy i.e., a change of subject.

Ben is cooling it. The word caliphate, meaning an Islamic State, is *low frequency* and not understood by everyone. It could be annoying. Also note the attempt to say there is confusion; a useful ploy to diversify a

There is lack of clarity.

Bill: I think we should try to negotiate with their leaders.

debate.

Bill does not address Bill's comments and *opens another debate.* The *straw man* technique again.

Ben: They will not agree to any negotiation at present. Have you not read the WikiLeaks Files? They complain continually of American and other Western interference in their country's affairs – especially in Syria and Iraq.

An *ex cathedra* statement 'they will not agree to any negotiation'. Has anyone tried to negotiate with their leaders? Reference to the Wikileaks files is a challenge as surprisingly few people have read them.

Bill: I've read part of the Wikileaks files. It is said that all violent disputes end by having to negotiate.

Never admit ignorance. It is best to say you have read some of the book in question. Good to *use a quote*- ideally from a famous person. It is fairly weak evidence here though.

Ben: Historically you are right but the person who wins the conflict always has the upper hand in negotiation.

Ben is showing off his wider knowledge of history. The debate appears to end in a draw.

3. DEATH OF PRINCESS DIANA IN 1997

This is a highly contentious event associated with multiple conspiracy theories. At the time, Diana had divorced from Prince Charles and was in a relationship with Dodi, the son of Mohamed Al Fayed, then owner of Harrods store in London. It is alleged that she was carrying Dodi's baby. She was trying to secure an international ban on anti-personnel mines and was in engaging in media activities that caused disquiet in British Royal circles and the Government. Some conspiracy theorists claim she was murdered by MI6 on the orders of the British Royal family with a staged accident in the Pont de l'Alma in Paris.

The mock interview below is an example of a 'demolition job' by interviewer 'Nick' of conspiracy theorist Fred.

Nick: We were all greatly saddened by the loss of Diana but surely you cannot be suggesting that she was in fact murdered.

A leading question as preferred by so many media interviewers.

Fred: I am, actually, and so do a lot of others.

A *generalisation* which would make him open to cross-examination. Also, just because a lot of people believe something does not automatically make it true – the *bandwagon fallacy*.

Nick: Perhaps you could be more specific?

Fred: There are several books written that support this theory.

Nick: Just because there are books written still does not give us solid evidence. What are the facts, Fred?

Fred: Diana's car was seen on CCTV to have been tampered with before she set off from the Ritz Hotel in Paris. The only people who could have opened her car would have been MI6.

Nick: But has there been identification of the supposed security officer who allegedly 'tampered' with her car? Could it not have been her driver checking out the car that evening?

Fred: He was asked and denied any such activity.

Nick: How could that have happened, I thought he died in the crash!

Fred: Sorry, you are right.

Nick: So what other 'evidence' do you have?

Fred: Diana's Mercedes was driven at speed pursued by the paparazzi and at the entrance of

Still vague. Circular reasoning makes him vulnerable...

Wielding the knife and asking for *evidence* – always the best form of attack.

Now some detail at last.

The ridicule approach.

More *ridicule.*

Admits mistake. Generally, a good tactic.

More *ridicule*

Use of *was thought to be* - a sign of weak argument.

the Pont de l'Alma there was a group of motor cyclists awaiting her arrival who followed her into the tunnel. This group was thought to be MI6 officers.

Nick: But was it not true that there were photographers all over the place and the first group say at the Ritz Hotel, could easily have phoned other paparazzi to reveal where the Mercedes was heading.

Drilling down for more detail which is a good tactic but the phrase '*was it not true*' can be a sign of weakness.

Fred: That is possible but immediately before the crash in the tunnel there was a blinding flash allegedly from a military grade laser that would have disorientated the driver.

Another weak phrase '*allegedly from*'.

Nick: But it was a dark evening, and there were photographers using flash all the time and in a tunnel a camera flash would surely illuminate everywhere.

Surely – a sign of minor weakness from Nick.

Fred: There was also a minor collision with a white Fiat that was never found until months later, totally burned out in an Italian military defence establishment.

Some evidence but source unspecified.

Nick: Anymore 'evidence'?

Nick is getting irritated.

Fred: The white Fiat was seen close to the Mercedes by a

A few scraps of evidence, but hardly compelling detail.

photographer who noted that the Fiat then left at great speed. This is documented in the French Police report.

Nick: At last, some proper evidence from the police report.

Fred: It is also suspected that MI6 interfered with the brakes and steering of the Mercedes, just before they set off from the hotel or at the tunnel entrance.

Repetition of an earlier point can be a sign of weakness. *it is also suspected* – another weak phrase.

Nick: We discussed that rather tenuous evidence earlier.

Hearsay evidence or verbiage as lawyers like to call it.

Fred: Also, I met a senior engineer who worked for Mercedes at the time who said the technology to interfere with the braking system remotely was definitely available even then and that the French authorities refused to release the car to Mercedes for inspection. He thought she was murdered.

Nick: But this engineer you bumped into may have already decided she was murdered and just used the technology 'evidence' to re-affirm his pre-conceptions. Just because the technology was available does not necessarily mean it was used. Did he testify to any of the

Nick is right. Only *circumstantial evidence* is produced. The engineer might be using *selective recall bias* or *myside bias*. Also, the sentence starting 'just because...' is an example of *post hoc ergo proctor hoc (after this therefore because of this)*. Association by possession does enquiries?

I think all your evidence is weak and circumstantial just like so many conspiracy theorists. Thank you, Fred.

not necessarily infer causation.

4. THE NATIONAL HEALTH SERVICE (NHS)

In the UK, health care is provided free of charge, although there are a few exceptions. Private health insurance is available for those who can afford it or who have this facility included in their salary – as offered by large corporations. The system works but there are multiple economic pressures and continual inroads from the private sector, raising concerns that the NHS one day may be privatised completely.

Cartoon pt 2.3

The following is a simulated interview by 'John' and the Minister of Health.

John: The NHS is clearly unaffordable isn't it Minister?

The usual *leading question*, but remember this is a senior politician who will have debated the topic multiple times, and will not be ruffled by this type of question.

Minister: Thank you for giving me the opportunity to answer this difficult question but before I do, I must emphasize that we are all going through a rough patch at present, and it very much depends on what you mean by 'unaffordable'.

The Minister is delaying his reply, trying to *define the terms* and *buying time*. Note: there is no point using low frequency words here. Ministers are professionals in debate.

John: We are all aware of the increasing numbers of elderly people and their demands on our stretched health resources and the situation is only going to get worse.

Minister: I fully appreciate the difficulties our health service is facing at present and there is no easy solution, but when you look at the big picture and compare our services with those elsewhere, the British people have a pretty good deal.

The Minister is avoiding an answer to the question. He is still playing for time while he thinks of a response, if forced to. He resorts to jargon: 'the *British People*'. This is generally a sign of weakness that often represents the user's own view. He could be attacked for not comparing *like with like,* that is, a comparison with a country of similar wealth.

John: But that's simply not good enough. You are supposed to be the person

John getting annoyed or pretending to be. *Showing motion or use of aggressive language* is a good tactic running the NHS are you not?

Minister: Well yes and no. I work in collaboration with several other ministers to provide overall guidance, for example to the Chief Medical Officer, Chief Social Work Officer, Chief Nursing Officer etc. I'm just one cog in the wheel and we are all responsible ultimately to Cabinet and the Prime Minister.

John: Well surely you can tell us *something* about what you might be thinking of to get us out of this mess?

Minister: We are minded to introduce a limited form of privatisation in certain key areas such as cataract surgery and hip surgery.

John: Perhaps you could be more explicit?

Minister: Given the high demand on NHS eye care and orthopaedic units for routine operations, we are thinking of offering this facility to the private sector so they will be able to enhance services to

sometimes as many people when angry may say things they regret subsequently.

Still stalling. *'yes and no'* is a favourite phrase of bureaucrats. Use of the 'cog in the wheel' *metaphor* is helpful as it can be easily redefined later if needed.

John getting really annoyed at this point and being *judgemental* with the last phrase which is a *leading question/statement.*

At last! *'minded to'* is a weasel phrase. Deliberately vague.

Asking for *evidence.* Always a powerful ploy.

Completely unruffled.

their patients.

John: Go on.

Minister: Well, that's it. We will build several special day units typically attached to large NHS hospitals. They will have their own separate staff and provide the necessary services.

John: So, who will benefit from all this?

Minister: The patients of course.

Getting ready to pounce.

John: What about the owners of the facility? They must be paid for their costs and clearly, would wish to make a profit?

Drilling down! Dagger drawn!

Minister: Of course, the providers of this service need to be compensated, and we shall be monitoring very closely the progress of this new venture to ensure that it is entirely commensurate with the public interest.

Note the studious avoidance of the word 'profit' and use of buzz words: 'service'; 'providers' and 'compensated'.

John: How will you ensure that the quality of surgery is adequate, staff pay is appropriate, sufficient number of doctors and nurses are recruited, and finally, Minister, in the register of member's

John makes the mistake of *firing multiple questions*. Reminiscent of the *'Gish gallop'*. The minister can now just pick off the ones he prefers to answer.

interests you are listed as a non-executive member of the very same company that you are promoting for this new venture apparently 'in the public interest'.

Minister: There will be a rigorous process of audit for all services offered and I shall take personal responsibility for the success of this venture.

He dodges the tricky one.

John: I'm sure you would, given that you are a member of the company's Board. Thank you, Minister.

John has not forgotten and ends with a final, crushing blow.

5. CLIMATE CHANGE

Although the majority of scientific evidence supports an unprecedented increase in global temperature there are still those who deny the concept. Here is a simulated interview between Cathy and a climate change denier, Andrew.

Cartoon Pt 2.4

Cathy: It is obvious that the unparalleled elevation of our planet's temperature relates to the greenhouse effect.

The usual *leading question* favoured by most interviewers.

Andrew: That's a popular concept and thank you for giving me the opportunity to respond to

Playing for time while he thinks of a good response

this important issue.

Cathy: So, what has led you to become a climate denier? What is the evidence?

Always a good attack - to *ask for evidence.*

Andrew: Well, there is evidence from history - of previous rises in global temperature like the warm period of the 13th century, and indeed the reverse - like the known ice ages and the more recent little ice age that happened between the 14th-18th centuries. It's only just finished and now we may be seeing a slight overswing. How did humans contribute to the ice-ages? There is evidence that the current global warming has slowed down, and that the apparent warming trend is secondary to urbanisation around weather stations – the 'urban heat island' effect. It is unlikely that the relatively small amounts of carbon dioxide produced by humans are relevant given the vast amounts produced by the oceans and volcanos.

Andrew is using the *'Gish Gallop'* defence. He makes multiple points in the hope it will overwhelm the interviewer. The presence of ice-ages might be viewed as *red-herrings* – certainly they are not directly relevant.

Cathy: You have made multiple points there but what is the actual solid scientific evidence that global temperatures are *not*

Unphased, she returns to the original point.

Undertones of *Karl Popper* in that Cathy requests falsifying rising?

Andrew: I have already given you plenty of evidence and on top of that, the climate change ideas are put forward just by the looney left, libertarians and democrats – all with various other axes to grand.

evidence.

Andrew is holding his ground without producing any scientific points and attempting to change the topic into the political arena. The *straw man* trick. He also tries to *pigeonhole* people with an opposite view – 'looney left' etc.

Cathy: Just because someone is left wing, or a libertarian doesn't mean they are necessarily wrong. Can you give me some actual data that supports your cause?

Remaining firm but polite.

Andrew: Well, there was that study by Professor Phil Jones the University of East Anglia (UEA) that claimed to show a rise in global temperature, but they concealed data that did not support their case and were thought to be fraudulent.

Some more concrete information at last.

Cathy: But ultimately further investigation into this matter – so-called 'Climategate' - revealed that there was no fraud at all and in the wake of that, a major US oil firm commissioned their own enquiry which corroborated the UEA findings. There are of course, many conflicts of interest; do you have any

Cathy is well briefed and raises the dagger!

conflicts you may wish to declare Fred?

Andrew: True, there was a small investigation after the UEA enquiry but the whole area is fraught with loose assumptions and counter assumptions.

Andrew is on the back foot and avoiding the conflicts question and trying to *change the subject.*

Cathy: Like what you might see on astroturfing web pages? So, do you, or do you not have, any conflicts of interest in this debate? Yes, or no?

He may not know what is *astroturfing* (a form of fake news. See Chapter 6) but will not wish to disclose his ignorance. Cathy uses a blunt *yes/no question* that can lead to angry denial etc.

Andrew: Well, I have received small amounts for lecturing on the topic.

Reluctant response.

Cathy: And who was it who paid you?

Wielding the knife! *Conflicts of interest* attack is a powerful weapon.

Andrew: A recent one was from Exxon.

Gotcha!

Cathy: That's a major oil company, isn't it? That explains a lot. Thank you, Fred.

She knew this all along but wanted to make him squirm as time ran out.

6. FEMALE GENITAL MUTILATION (FGM)

This is a highly emotive issue with most Western societies strongly against it. The mock debate below is between a neutral TV interviewer (Karen) and an African proponent, (Fatima).

Karen: As we both know this is a highly contentious issue but how can you possibly condone FGM for anyone, anywhere?

The usual *leading question* for opening a debate.

Fatima: I agree the matter is highly controversial but in Africa we believe that it is the correct thing to do in young females. We also prefer the term female circumcision (FC) as there is no mutilation when it is done correctly, and it is a safe procedure in the right hands. There is also the matter of cultural relativism.

Defining the terms of the debate correctly. Use of the *low frequency phrase* 'cultural relativism' implies a high level of education and possibly puts Karen on the back foot as she may not have come across the term.

Karen: How can you possibly say that? What is the evidence that FC is 'correct' and what do you actually mean by cultural relativism?

Asking for *evidence*. Always a good strategy. Karen conceals her ignorance by *asking what do you actually mean by* 'cultural relativism'. A clever tactic.

Fatima: In Africa we believe that FC makes a girl spiritually clean and more chaste. In the 'Hadith' – that is, sayings attributed to

Fatima has the upper hand here but avoids being condescending. An excellent tactic - as long as you want a friendly debate.

Muhammad, it is praised as noble but not mandatory. However, it is obligatory in the Shafi'i version of Sunni Islam. It also helps ensure that she remains a virgin until she marries. Cultural relativism refers to the idea that beliefs, values and practices should be understood in the context of an individual's own culture rather than against criteria of another say, Western, culture.

Karen: But that's a belief, do you have evidence of benefit for this?

Special pleading in a sense. This is an act of faith and therefore the rules of logic may not apply. Little evidence of benefit is supplied apart from religious doctrine.

Fatima: Most parents seeking FC for their daughters are devout Muslims and as I stated earlier, FC may be undertaken at parents' request.

The counter argument.

Karen: But there are all sorts of risk involved – such as extreme pain, bleeding and infection that may affect a girl's subsequent fertility, let alone her mental state.

Fatima: That is true but only when the procedure is undertaken by someone unqualified, usually in secrecy because of the major opposition to it in the Western world. When it is performed under sterile conditions there is no discomfort and very few risks. Our religion does not condemn FC and it is not against the law as it is in the West.

Karen: But what possible benefits are conferred by FC? I have heard of nothing but harm.

Karen is on the back foot: '*I have heard' is* a sign of weakness in debate.

Fatima: The benefits are chiefly religious as I have explained.

Karen: Then I presume for the UK you would be in favour of legalising FC so that anyone who wished to have it done on their daughter could do so at least as a safe procedure? Most people would not support this view even as a medically safe procedure.

Karen is using the '*bandwagon fallacy'* approach given that opinion in UK is strongly against FC and doctors are not permitted to undertake it. '*Most people'* is a weak statement and it is liable to attack by someone with accurate data.

Fatima: I am aware of the ban on FC in the UK but what about male circumcision?

Changing the subject perhaps? Could be viewed as a *straw man* diversion but quite legitimate.

Karen: That's a completely different matter.

Fatima: No, it is not! In most situations a baby boy is circumcised at the wish of the parents for purely religious

Good response. It is important to '*compare like with like'.*

reasons – typically by Arabs and Jews. Very rarely is it required for medical conditions. There are religious reasons for both procedures. Both are safe when undertaken by someone with the correct training.

Karen: So you would be in favour of legalising FC in the West as long as it was undertaken by appropriately qualified people?

Leading question again but it gets Karen nowhere in the debate.

Fatima: Yes – that is correct.

Karen: FC is not easily reversible, so what if a young adult female who had FC as a baby or child decides later that she would have preferred not to have it done?

Changing the subject slightly with the implicit argument that if FC is not easily reversible, it should not be done.

Fatima: I agree that is a difficult situation but no different from an adult circumcised male.

Inescapable logic, but *two wrongs do not make a right.*

Karen: In essence you are supporting FC for any religious parents who wish that to be performed on their daughters? But what about the human rights of the child?

Karen has a good point about human rights and now changes the subject.

Fatima: It's exactly the same debate for circumcision in males. The only argument *against* FC is where it is done by unqualified people.

Karen: As long as you accept the somewhat tenuous religious justification for it in the first place. Thank you, Fatima. Debate closes with a draw! That is all you can hope for in matters of deeply held religious views and practice.

7. ABORTION LAW

The laws governing abortion vary widely across the world. Some countries have an outright ban. Others impose restrictions but most of the Western World, Russia, China and Australasia have adopted a liberal view permitting termination on request. Grounds for ending a pregnancy include threats to the mother's life; her physical or mental health; rape; significant foetal abnormalities; economic and social reasons. Here is a mock debate between two opposing parties: Brenda – a lay person against abortion and Brian, who is medically qualified and in favour

Brenda: Most people believe that terminating the life of an unborn child is wrong and nothing short of murder of a defenceless person.

Clear opening statement of the anti-abortion view. *'Most people believe'* is a weak statement if there are no statistics in support.

Brian: In many respects I totally agree with you, but a lot depends on what you mean by 'life'.

Brian is using the *'Socratic jujitsu'* approach. Beware of debaters who start off by agreeing with you. However, he is *establishing the terms of debate* by clarifying Brenda's interpretation of the word 'life'.

Brenda: By life I mean something that begins at the moment of successful fertilization.

Brian: So would you say that on day 3 for example – the morula stage where there are only 16

Brian is starting a slow demolition job!

cells – this still represents 'life'?

Brenda: I do.

Brian: I am sure you are aware of alternative definitions of 'life'. Apart from yours, there is a scientific one that describes it as the ability to sustain an independent existence. Others define life as the time at which a baby's heartbeat can be detected by vaginal ultrasound. There is another definition that states life begins at 26 weeks because that is the earliest time a baby can survive if removed from the womb. This assumes the baby is cared for by the mother and medical staff. In one sense even a healthy new-born baby is not capable of an independent existence because it is dependent on its mother or its family for food. A new-born baby is not able to forage for nutrition on its own until it is much older.

Patronising response that is likely to annoy, but agreement on the terms of debate is essential.

Brenda: You're not suggesting that it's OK to terminate the life of a new-born baby just because it doesn't obey your definition of independent life! I am aware of alternative definitions, but I re-iterate that my definition is clear.

Fighting back with ridicule! Also personalising the debate ('your definition') – a technique that may annoy.

Brian: that's certainly a tenable

Again, appearing to agree again,

view that a lot of people would support but what is the basis for it?

and using the third-party approach – *'a lot of people would support'*. No hard facts are offered such as results from surveys.

Brenda: It's partly from fundamental moral principles and my philosophy of life.

Note that there is no declared recourse to religious principles. If your opponent is deeply religious, you are unlikely to change their view because of *circular reasoning* and *special pleading.*

Brian: So, what are the particular moral principles that you follow in this context.

Dissecting out the foundations of this belief.

Brenda: Those of kindness, compassion, actions for the common good and the sanctity of human life.

Brian: I agree with all of that but in the case of termination of pregnancy you are dealing with two 'lives', where only one person can voice an opinion, but the mother may also be sincerely guided by her own moral values just like you.

Again, *appearing to agree.* Beware of this tactic!

Brenda: I believe that the mother is responsible for both her own life and that of her baby and has no right to end either.

'I believe' is usually a sign of weakness. Also, the word 'right' has little legal value unless embodied in the Human Rights Act.

Brian: So, she would have no right to commit suicide in any circumstances?

Attempting to '*extreme*' the debate.

Brenda: Again, that is correct.

Brian: Are you aware of the link between terminations of pregnancy and crime rate?

Digging deeper and hoping that Brenda is not familiar

Brenda: I may have heard of it briefly.

It is *never wise to admit ignorance* as your opponent may be tempted to say almost anything from the quoted source.

Brian: This was proposed by Levitt and Dubner in their book 'Freakonomics'. They point out the high rates of crime (including homicide) by those born because of unwanted pregnancies and conclude that although abortion takes away one unwanted life it may subsequently *save* lives in future by lowering murder rates in society.

A somewhat controversial idea and horrific to many, despite the compelling statistics in support provided by the authors! Brian *throws a dead cat on the table*. It's probably not a good tactic to bring out an idea that you know will be rejected outright - unless you wish to humiliate your opponent.

Brenda: That's absolutely dreadful! You are exchanging one innocent life on the remote possibility of saving someone else's life in future. That is one of the worst proposals to bring down crime I have ever heard.

Predictable response. The possibility is not remote however, it is based on real life statistics.

Brian: OK. So, what if the foetus is found on ultrasound of the

Anencephaly refers to a baby without a head. A *low frequency* womb to have anencephaly? Would you permit a termination in this context where the baby will die at birth? Does quality of life not have a role?

Brenda: Quality of life is important, but I believe there is no moral right to take away a life even though subsequent death at birth is inevitable.

Brian: Would you have the same view if the mother had severe depression, if she had conceived through rape, or had a severe cardiac condition that could result in her death and that of her child, through continuation of the pregnancy?

word that could ruffle an opponent.

Brenda: I would.

Brian: But earlier you mentioned the importance of kindness, compassion, and actions for the common good.

The dagger is drawn! Using the *'extreme it'* attack.

Brenda: Surely it is wrong to take away an innocent life and there is still the possibility of a reasonably healthy baby.

The dagger is plunged but the 'sanctity of human life' aspect is omitted.

Brian: So if we go back to an extreme case – which does happen occasionally - where the mother has a severe heart condition, has been raped and her

Use of the word *'surely'* is a sign of weakness. Brenda is simply re-iterating her earlier statement. All anencephalics die.

Huntington's disease usually starts in middle age and characterised by jerky limb movements, unsteadiness and a progressive dementia. It affects baby has the gene for Huntington's disease, confirmed by chorionic villous sampling, would you still allow the pregnancy to proceed, where the risk of death to both mother and child were high and even if the child survived it would succumb to an unpleasant dementing condition in middle age. How does this fit with your belief of kindness, compassion and actions for the common good?

Brenda: I still think that even in this tragic situation the immorality of murdering an unborn child is greater than the competing morality allowing the pregnancy to continue despite the dreadful risks. In any event there are substantial risks to abortion.

Brian: You may be right on that. Perhaps you could remind me what are the risks for legal termination of pregnancy compared to similar procedures such as childbirth itself?

Brenda: I don't know any exact figures, but I've read that it carries risk of infection, severe bleeding and infertility.

Brian: The US Centers for Disease

50% of children born from an affected parent. The chorion is part of the womb that may be sampled safely during pregnancy to determine whether the Huntington gene is present in the baby. If this gene is present the disease is inevitable.

Brian is using the *extreme case* scenario to once more counter Brenda's 'philanthropic' beliefs.

Brenda holds her ground and then tries to *change the subject* (Straw Man tactic).

Brian sets double trap by *appearing to agree* and using a *rhetorical question* to which he knows the answer. Vacuum aspiration is a routine procedure used to extract foetal contents up to the 14th week.

Weak reply: *'I've read that'*.

Solid facts like these are hard to

Control & Prevention (CDC) estimated that in 2019, there were overall 17.2 maternal deaths/100,000 live births, compared to 0.7/maternal deaths per 100,000 abortions. Where terminations are undertaken in approved healthcare facilities, abortion is safe. Do you not agree? Also, there is the other equally safe option of hormonally induced termination with tablets.

Brenda: I accept your point on safety but not accept your argument about the morality which infringes the basic human rights of an unborn child.

deny if you do not know any figures yourself.

The debate ends with an amicable draw.

8. POLICE RACIAL PREJUDICE FOR STOP AND SEARCH

In many countries, the police have the power to stop and search anyone they have reasonable grounds to think has broken the law or about to do so. The police are frequently accused of racial discrimination but is it justified? What follows is a mock debate between an interviewer, Rosemary, and Michael a senior member of the police force in London (The 'Met').

Note that some of the 'evidence' provided may not be completely accurate. The discussion is principally to exemplify various debating techniques.

Cartoon Pt 2.5

Rosemary: It's beyond any reasonable doubt that the Met is racially prejudiced towards people of colour is it not?

The usual *leading question* – which is unlikely to ruffle a senior police officer.

Michael: Well, thank you for raising this important question, but before I do, could you tell me how you are defining 'people of colour'?

Two *stalling responses* but quite rightly *asking for clarification* of this term. Otherwise, the debate can quickly revolve around cross purposes. Semantics are so important!

Rosemary: I think most people know what I mean but shall we focus on say Blacks – that is Afro-Caribbean.

Now changing the grounds of debate slightly.

Michael: Do you mean Blacks born in the UK or Blacks of Afro-Caribbean descent? That is, with parents of Afro-Caribbean origin or 'ethnicity'.

Further clarification requested.

Rosemary: Let's include both Blacks born in UK and those of Black ethnicity. So, can you now tell us why Blacks as we have now defined are more likely to be stopped and searched?

The *terms are now defined* better. It is so important to clarify the terms in a debate.

Again, there is a *leading question* which should not cause a problem with an experienced interviewee.

Michael: I'm sure you have read the latest documents from the Met.

Good tactics. A *rhetorical question* and he is implying he is in full possession of the relevant facts.

Rosemary: Yes, I have read some of

Also, good tactics. *Never*

them.

Michael: Well as you will know, there were 375,588 stop and searches in England and Wales from April 2018-March 2019 which represented a significant downward trend.

Rosemary: A fall from what to what?

Michael: The stop and search rate has fallen by 18% since 2010. We have made really good progress I believe.

Rosemary: Is 18% a relative or absolute figure?

Michael: I'm not sure what you mean. Perhaps you could explain.

Rosemary: Can you tell me about the raw data for the improvement you are claiming?

Michael: If I may look at my notes. Ah yes, in 2009-2010 there were 25 stop and searches per 1000 people compared to 7 stop and searches for 2018-2019 which is an 18% reduction as I said.

admit ignorance. Best to say you have read part of a book/document etc. even if it's just the introduction!

Solid figures but trying to avoid the central issue which is whether Blacks are stopped more often than Whites.

Drilling down for detail.

Use of *percentages* (almost always relative rather than absolute) is a widespread practice but beware of someone familiar with statistics.

She is familiar with basic statistics and uses this to see if it humiliates Michael.

Major point scored!

She avoids humiliation of a senior figure. Never a bad idea.

On the back foot here.

Rosemary: So, your 18% represents a <u>relative</u> risk reduction from 2.5% to 0.7% but the <u>absolute</u> rate is a mere 1.8%. Some would say that's not very impressive for a period of 8-9 years. Basically, it means that for every 100 potential arrests you have reduced the stop and search numbers by a mere 2 people!

Michael does not understand *the difference between relative and absolute risks*, so a major point is scored here.

Also note that Rosemary uses the *third person* i.e., 'some would say'. This avoids making the debate too heated and personal.

Michael: I admit the changes are not massive, but they are in the right direction and the problem is not easy to deal with. However, if you extrapolate the findings to the Black population in London that represents nearly 18,000 fewer arrests for every million Black people – which is not too bad.

Partial admission of failure?

However, he quickly calculates the effect on the wider population and thus paints a better picture than the simple percentage calculations would infer. He finishes with *understatement* which is usually a good strategy.

Rosemary: OK so now let's deal with the specifics of racial prejudice. The Met have been accused of institutional racism and using stop and search tactics on Blacks far more often than Whites. Is that not correct?

Michael: I do admit there is a problem, but we are tackling it vigorously. If you look at the latest stop and search figures, there were 114,982 Whites and 122,492 Blacks apprehended in the 12-month period up to May 2020. That's

It is a frequent response to say that a given problem is under close scrutiny, but here are some solid figures.

48.4% White and 51.6% Black. So, the figures are not that far apart.

Rosemary: Well, if you use simple percentages that might be the case but if you look at the raw data that's 7,510 more Blacks in just one year and we are not talking about the additional 51,257 Asians who were stopped in the same period. If you add these up that's nearly 60,000 more people of colour who are stopped and searched because they were of the 'wrong' colour. Surely you cannot deny there is not a problem here?

Good points.

She deviates slightly from the problem by Including Asians. Not quite a *straw man* approach.

Use of the word *'surely'* often denotes weakness.

Also, there is a *double negative* 'cannot deny' and 'is not' which add up to a positive.

Michael: I agree the figures are not so good if you include Asians, but we agreed to focus on Blacks. It is important to compare like with like.

Good strategy *'like with like'*.

Rosemary: I'm not sure what you mean.

Michael: Well, you have to match Whites and Blacks according to their living conditions, health, employment status, average income etc. Also, you must compare the total number of Blacks and Whites in a given community or at very least make adjustments for any inequality. It's quite possible that Blacks appear to commit more crime because there are just more of them, let alone the issues around

Good points.

social deprivation which is more prevalent in Blacks.

Rosemary: But the vast majority of crime related to stop and search is connected with drug possession and related crime. Surely, you're not implying that shortage of illegal drugs is a cause of social deprivation.

Use of *ridicule*. This may gain the upper hand at the risk of alienating your opponent.

Michael: Of course, I agree with that. What is needed is a head-to-head comparison of Blacks and Whites matched by number, age, social circumstances etc.

He is referring to a *case-control study*. His argument is looking good.

Rosemary: Has one been done?

Michael, I'm afraid not, and until we have such an investigation the possibility of racial bias in the Met will remain an open question.

Rosemary: So, you don't think there is bias at all?

Pushing hard for any crack in his armour.

Michael: There may be, but until we have a properly matched case-control study we will never know for sure.

Debate ends as a friendly draw.

9. CAPITAL PUNISHMENT

Many Western countries still impose the death penalty for intentional murder (and other serious offences), but over the last 100 years it has been replaced gradually by less severe sentences, usually life imprisonment. Here is a mock debate between a Libertarian, Toby, who is in favour of abolition and a prison officer, Gary, who wants to keep it.

Note that some of the 'evidence' provided may not be completely accurate. The discussion is principally to exemplify various debating techniques.

Cartoon Pt 2.6

Toby: In my view the death penalty for murder is outmoded and barbaric, achieves nothing in terms of crime prevention, risks killing the innocent and appeals to the worst aspects of human nature – namely schadenfreude. How can you possibly support it? Res ipsa loquitor, surely.

He makes about five separate points here - akin to the *'Gish gallop'*.

Not a good way to start a debate but some like this approach in the hope of overwhelming their opponent. He may think that because of Gary's occupation he will be a weak adversary and resorts to a *low frequency word* (schadenfreude – grim pleasure in revenge) and then a *Latin phrase*- res ipsa loquitor – 'the facts speak for themselves'.

Gary: Well, you've made a lot of points there so let's start with your first contention that it is outmoded and barbaric. It depends on what you mean by 'outmoded' but if by this you imply something that is not fashionable in the West then you should look no further than the US. As you know the death penalty is still practised in 28 of 50 States to this day and there is no sign that it is going to be abolished. Indeed, surveys suggest that the public are in favour of retaining it. Certainly, the death penalty was barbaric 300-400 years ago when there were public

Toby had not realised he was up against a tough opponent! Gary rightly wishes to *clarify the term* 'outmoded' – but leaves alone 'barbaric'. He knows relevant figures about the USA.

executions but now it is more humane with death by lethal injection, electrocution, rarely hanging, firing squad or lethal gas.

Toby: I am aware that capital punishment is still practised widely in some Western countries. Public executions were practised in Florida and Utah right until 1992, but that does not make it morally acceptable. Furthermore, many states in the USA are trying to abolish the death penalty forever. In 2018, Pew's polls showed diminishing support for the death penalty from 80% in 1974 to 49% in 2016. Are you in favour of capital punishment for juveniles as well?

He makes the point that *universality of practice* does not necessarily make an action acceptable. This is the *bandwagon fallacy*. He cites figures to cement his case and ends with a highly emotive change of subject – death sentences for juveniles! The *straw man tactic* given that it is easier to demolish arguments in favour of juvenile rather than adult capital punishment.

Gary: You have cherry-picked the polls that support your case. In the USA, the Lake Research Partners poll in 2010 found that 61% preferred the death penalty for murder. In 2009 a Gallup poll found that 77% of Americans thought that the masterminds behind the 911 attacks should be executed.

Solid data but who is being more selective?

The approach is reminiscent of *'Myside Bias'.*

Far more detail from both sides is required.

Toby: It is true that not all polls point in the same direction but there are important trends in public opinion that suggest there is a gradual shift toward abolition. You have not responded to my juvenile's point. Why not?

Good to concede this point as it helps to lower the temperature of debate – temporarily! Toby knows that execution of juveniles is highly contentious.

Gary: The question of juveniles is more difficult but on balance I'm in not in favour of the death penalty for them.

Toby: In the US, children under the age of 16 are not executed but in some Westernised countries it is permitted. For example, in Japan a man was executed in 2017 for a crime he committed at the age of 18y. How can you support capital punishment for adults and not children? When does a person become responsible for their actions? Age 5, 10, 15, puberty?

Not such a good counter argument given that the age of the person hanged in Japan was 18y and arguably an adult. It is purely *anecdotal information* and thus liable to be demolished easily.

Gary: I don't know the exact age.

On the back foot. Time to *create a diversion? Throw a dead cat on the table – or knock something over?*

Toby: if you do not know the age of responsibility then how can you make any moral judgement? What about

Toby is using the *extreme it* ploy to good effect here

someone of 20y or 25y – or a 30y old with low intelligence or psychiatric history? What about an 80y old with dementia? Some countries do not execute the very elderly especially if they are sick.

Gary: I agree the situation is complex and they say such punishment is wrong, but I am really talking about adults.

Back-tracking. Note use of the *'they'* word which usually denotes ignorance of solid facts. Gary attempts to change back to the original subject of adult execution.

Toby: How can it be right to murder a 20y old but not to kill a 17y old if they are both found guilty of identical pre-meditated homicide.

Toby keeps up the pressure. Comparing *like with like* (almost). A powerful tactic

Gary: I don't know. You also mention the ineffectiveness of capital punishment on crime prevention. This is incorrect.

Gary now tries a different tactic. *Straw man again.*

Toby: Well, give me some figures then.

Fine to ask for data as long as you have your own figures.

Gary: There have been several studies including those by Dezhbakhsh and Rubin (2011) and Zimmerman (2009) who found a mild but definite deterrent effect on the rate of crime, particularly in the few months after a local prison

Good evidence but it may well be selective. *My side bias* again.

execution.

Toby: It is my understanding that some studies do show a deterrent effect but there are several that show no effect at all.

'it is my understanding'. Generally, a sign of weakness in debate

Gary: It is true that many experts disagree. But what if the death penalty *were* abolished for all homicides? The prisons would then fill up with murderers – who would increase demands on staff, finance etc. Also, someone who previously should have been executed for murder would be free in prison to commit further assassinations as he is already there for life.

Gary is using the *'extreme it'* method again.

His second point is good basic logic .

Toby: Is there any evidence that re-offending happens frequently in prisoners on life-sentences for murder? It all boils down to two issues really. The lack of good scientific evidence for and against the death penalty and whether other measures such as rehabilitation might work instead. We are in a state of equipoise and research should be directed at solving the problem once and for all.

An over-simplification with *use of a low frequency word* equipoise (ignorance) that he hopes might bamboozle Gary, but no such luck!

Gary: So, if future research, say a well-designed case-control study, proved that the death penalty had a deterrent effect would you then support it?

He retaliates with a display of epidemiological knowledge (*case-control study*), thus rattling Toby .

Toby: Well, I really cannot support capital punishment in any shape or form.

He is a libertarian with unshakable core beliefs.

Gary: So, your mind is made up and there is really no point in debate as you would not abide by the conclusions of scientific research whether now or in the future.

More points to Gary here. Toby's values are akin to a religion where his final defence might be *'special pleading'* – that is, a situation where logic is replaced by the demands of firmly held moral or religious beliefs.

10. STREET BEGGING

Nearly all countries have a problem with street beggars. Some are passive, others request money aggressively, some just sleep rough and do not beg. Here is a mock three-sided debate between Tony, the interviewer, Doreen, a representative from a charity for homeless people and the parliamentary Minister responsible for housing.

Note that some of the 'evidence' provided may not be completely accurate. The discussion is principally to exemplify various debating techniques.

Cartoon Pt 2.7

Tony: Street begging has got out of control. Every time I set off to work, I am besieged by beggars some of whom get quite aggressive. What is your party doing about this rising problem?

The usual opening with a *leading question* that will never fool a member of parliament (MP). It is assumed there is a rising problem.

Minister: Thank you for giving me the opportunity for addressing this problem which we do, of course, take very seriously.

Playing for time.

Tony: So, what are you doing about it then?

Trying to keep on the subject.

Minister: It really depends on what you mean by begging. There is passive begging, aggressive begging and just people who sleep rough and cause little problem to others.

Once more *playing for time* and correctly asking for *clarity* of the topic under review.

Tony: Well, let's start with non-aggressive begging in the street. As I understand it, the level of that has gone up markedly.

Clarity established but the use of a phrase like *'as I understand it'* usually conveys ignorance of facts. Tony has perhaps inadvertently *changed the subject* slightly from 'what are you going to do about it' to 'the level has gone up markedly'. Politicians love this as they can pick off whichever topic suits them better.

Minister: Well, that's not the question. What really matters is what are the beggars doing there

Standard mode of defence: *attack the question!*

in the first place. I think most are scroungers looking to supplement their social benefits that taxpayers provide for them already. It's a burgeoning industry. I know of one man in Lincoln who begs in the city centre, who is not homeless at all, but regularly makes more than £50 a day from passers-by.

Doreen: How dare you say that! Just political mantra. Most street beggars are homeless people with multiple social problems, drug addiction, financial problems, chronic illness, and malnutrition, primarily a result of your inadequate social housing investment, year on year.

Tony: Let's stick to one item at a time. **Minister:** do you or Doreen know how many beggars in London for example, are 'scroungers' as you call them?

Minister: Regrettably there are no reliable figures available – even from the police who should be documenting this situation thoroughly.

Tony: This is unbelievable. Here we have a major social problem and neither of you can produce any reliable figures other than a

There is a further change of subject.

Use of *low frequency word* - burgeoning – (flourishing) is unlikely to ruffle Tony.

The example from Lincoln is true but an isolated example and should be attacked at once!

Slightly aggressive stance that may alienate the others. *Mantra* is a low frequency word (meaning a political slogan) that again is unlikely to confuse either party. Yet another potential change of subject and the anecdote has gone unchallenged.

Back on track maybe and now asking for evidence – the best form of attack.

Actually, this may be true at least for the UK.

Raising the temperature. Effects can be unpredictable.

few isolated stories that make headline news. How do you respond to Doreen's comments?

Minister: Our government has increased the housing budget every year since we took office. For example, the rate of new house building in London has gone up last year by 20%

Signal to attack if you understand percentages, like Doreen.

Doreen: That's nothing at all! In the year before then, the housing programme was virtually stagnant. So, an increase by 20% from just 2000 new builds represents a mere 400 extra houses and most of them were for the well-heeled leaving around 40 extra in the affordable category. So, are you suggesting we cram dozens of additional families into just 40 new properties?

Doreen has the *figures* to hand, always a reliable form of attack. She then uses *ridicule* to humiliate the Minister. Such approach is rarely successful with an experienced politician and may backfire.

Minister: We are working very hard to address this problem which is really more about creating hostels for the homeless rather than residential property.

'Working very hard': a favourite, mostly meaningless response of politicians. Another slight change of subject.

Doreen: I'm pleased to hear your department is working so hard, but what else would taxpayers expect you to be doing – slouching all day – just like the beggars you accuse of doing?

Ridicule again. Not always the best way to get results, but remember that an angry debater may be indiscreet, so this approach can be helpful.

Tony: Let's get back to the main

Restores order, fortunately for

topic. According to government figures in 2018 there were 4,677 people sleeping rough in England. Minister?

Minister: I accept that begging is a failure of society and that the rate is unacceptably high.

We are striving to increase the penalties for beggars, especially the aggressive variety.

Appearing to agree can be a danger signal. Reminiscent of so-called *'Socratic Jujitsu'!* Honesty can create support if sincere.

Doreen: I presume you are referring to the Vagrancy Act (1824)? It's just not working. There was one beggar in Manchester who was arrested nearly 100 times. He got fined and then had to beg more to pay the penalty. It is surely wrong to criminalise homelessness?

Doreen shows her knowledge of the law. She then resorts to an *anecdote,* which potentially is a feeble approach. Use of the word *'surely'* implies weakness as well.

Minister: Application of the Vagrancy Act is declining significantly and suggests that the matter is coming under control.

Appearing to agree with Doreen. Possible *circular reasoning.*

Doreen: I don't think so. It's simply that the Act does not correct the problem, so judges have not bothered to enforce it. You can take no reassurance whatsoever from a declining application of the Act.

She is right.

Tony: So, minister, what are your thoughts for improving the

the Minister.

situation?

Minister: We are taking the matter very seriously and have set up a working party which is due to report their findings quite soon.

'Setting up a working party' is *Civil Service code for delay* or doing nothing. Reports can take years to complete and then a different political party may be in power.

Tony: How soon is soon?

He knows this tactic

Minister: It is my understanding that it will be ready for review within the current parliamentary session

It is my understanding. Again, a sign of weakness or attempt to dodge the real truth.

Tony: Well, could one of you tell me exactly how you are going to improve the situation right now in view of the likely delayed government's report? Doreen.

An apparently innocent question.

Doreen: We are increasing pressure on our MPs and eagerly awaiting the results of the report.

Somewhat feeble response.

Tony: So, neither of you have any clear plan on what should be done right now! Meanwhile we continue to be embarrassed and appalled by the number of street beggars that neither of you seem capable of correcting?

A variant of the *'divide and rule'* approach where apparently neither party has thought through their problem convincingly.

Thank you both.

11. AMERICAN IMPERIALISM & TORTURE

Many countries have complained about a tendency for the USA to interfere with their internal affairs. This situation seems to go back to the Monroe Doctrine, delineated by President Monroe in 1823. It was implemented originally to resist any attempt of European powers to regain control of Central or South America. There have been several re-interpretations of the Doctrine which now is often taken to mean that that anything that happens in America's 'backyard', or indeed in any country that might have an adverse effect on America, is 'of interest' to the USA. The debate below moves on to the question of torture.

What follows is an imaginary debate between an American supporter of the Monroe doctrine (Mitch) and a left-wing interviewer from the UK (Phil).

Cartoon Pt 2.8

Phil: I gather you are a strong supporter of the Monroe doctrine, is that correct?

Mitch: Indeed, I am and I believe that this doctrine has materially contributed to the safety of our great country.

Phil: Perhaps one of the most formidable tests of the doctrine was the Cuban missile crisis in 1962.

Mitch: I certainly agree that was a tough time and a major challenge of John F Kennedy's powers of diplomacy and negotiation.

Phil: Many people regard Kennedy's threat to block and if needed attack the Russian fleet approaching Cuba as reckless and to have risked a major, possible nuclear war between two superpowers.

Careful *use of the third person* 'many people'.

Mitch: Well, Kennedy won that debate, and the Russians withdrew.

Ends justifies the means approach. Also, an example of *circular reasoning.*

Phil: Many people are not aware that in the months before the Cuban missile crisis America had installed several nuclear launch pads in Turkey and Italy which obviously, would be directed at Russia and thus infringing a hypothetical Russian 'Monroe' doctrine. Also, the Cubans were concerned about any repeat of the Bay

Gentle warm up.

Again, good *use of the third person* 'many people'. Cold logic throughout. In the Bay of Pigs incident, Cuban exiles funded by the CIA attempted a coup of the Cuban Castro regime which was unsuccessful.

of Pigs invasion that might infringe their sovereignty. Thus, the Cuban/Russian intention could be viewed as a reciprocal move to place nuclear weapons close to your soil just as you had done in Turkey and Italy.

Mitch: You're not comparing like with like here. America was seriously concerned about Russian expansionism into European countries on their western border.

The *like with like* defence.

Phil: just like America's unsuccessful attempts to colonise Cuba?

The *reciprocal* attack.

Mitch: Sovereignty of the USA must be protected at all costs and Cuba was just too close to our mainland to ignore.

Starting to go round in circles?

Phil: Even if that risks all out nuclear warfare?

Mitch: Well, it all ended peacefully when Khrushchev withdrew.

Mitch sidesteps the real issue. *Circular reasoning:* we must have been right because we won the confrontation.

Phil: Let's move on to the question of torture. This was defined quite clearly by the UN General Assembly in 1994 and yet the US, and indeed several other countries engage in torture. How do you respond to this?

This is correct: Article 1 of the UN General Assembly 1994 prohibits torture according to their definition.

Mitch: The US does not torture, nor

do we condone anyone who practises torture.

Phil: Apart from Guantanamo, may I remind you of the case of Chelsea Manning who in 2013 leaked cables from your State department listing episodes of torture in Iraq. He (Chelsea) was subsequently arrested and tortured himself.

An uncomfortable piece of US history.

Mitch: Manning was found guilty of treason and imprisoned for his crimes. He was not tortured

Avoids answering the basic accusation - torture in Iraq.

Phil: Well, how do you define torture?

The importance of *defining terms.*

Mitch: The UN article prohibits the use of 'severe pain'. It is never inflicted intentionally although subjects may inflict discomfort on themselves.

Mitch dodges the real point.

Phil: A lot rests on how you would define 'severe pain'. I suppose waterboarding would not be included in 'severe pain'.

Defining terms again. It is so important to debate.

Mitch: I agree that is difficult and a possible grey area.

At least some concession which is always a good response in heated debate.

Phil: But you must be aware of the vast amount of psychological literature that has all manner of analogue scales to quantify pain severity. And of course, people who have been waterboarded are petrified.

Factually correct.

Although they are not in 'physical' pain they certainly are in 'mental' pain.

Mitch: I am aware of some of the literature but surely you are not suggesting that prisoners are given psychological tests of how painful a particular procedure felt. That would be meaningless.

Phil: I'm not, but you could refer to prior investigations (if they exist) to justify non-painful procedures to extract information.

Never admit ignorance. An attempt at *ridicule* here. Dodges the waterboarding issue.

Mitch: this has not been done and I repeat the US does not condone or undertake torture on its soil.

Phil: so, you appear to be confirming why so many tortures have taken place in Guantanamo Bay, an area chosen deliberately because it is outside US legal jurisdiction. Thank you, Mitch .

A final blow perhaps.

12. VACCINATION

This is a highly emotive topic for some people, especially those without a formal medical or scientific training. There is a strong movement, usually led by those known as 'anti-vaxxers' that was given added impetus by claims from Andrew Wakefield, former gastro-enterologist at the Royal Free Hospital, London. In 1998 he suggested there was a link between the measles/mumps/rubella (MMR) vaccine and autism. His findings, published in The Lancet, were subsequently found to be fraudulent and retracted formally. Also, he was discovered to have several conflicts of interest. His name was subsequently removed from the UK Medical Register (held by the General Medical Council) yet he still attracts widespread media publicity.

This mock debate is between Frank, a scientist and Vera a prominent anti-vaxxer

Cartoon Pt 2.9

Frank: We have had vaccines for over 200 years and admittedly there have been hiccups, but surely now the evidence in favour of vaccination is overwhelming, given that they have virtually eradicated diphtheria, measles mumps, rubella, tetanus, polio, smallpox etc.

Clear statement.

Vera: I completely disagree. There are multiple problems with vaccines especially safety issues

Frank: Which vaccine are you referring to? The vast majority have a high safety profile as I'm sure you know.

This is a subtle trap by Frank - *'as I'm sure you know'*. He is goading Vera about safety. To use this approach, you must know the figures and hope your opponent does not!

Vera: Well, what about the Cutter incident of 1955 with the Salk vaccine for polio. There were 40,000 cases of polio, 200 instances of paralysis and 10 deaths. That's pretty damning, isn't it?

Major point. There was a fault in production that resulted in live polio virus being given. Solid facts are always a trump card. Just because this vaccine was unsafe does not mean that all others are risky. A form of Myside bias.

Frank: You are absolutely right, that was a tragedy, but it has led to tighter scrutiny of the pharmaceutical industry and replacement by an attenuated vaccine. This all happened many years ago. We've moved on since.

He refers to the Sabin vaccine which is safer.

Use of a low frequency word 'astroturfing' (a form of online fake news) can aid an attack.

Things are much safer now despite loads of astroturfing.

Vera: Well, what about the MMR vaccine and the link to autism.

Change of subject / Straw Man defence.

Frank: Surely you must know the background to this and the fact that Dr Wakefield was discredited.

Vera: Of course, I know, but there was a massive government and pharmaceutical driven lobby to discredit the association. They were all significantly conflicted – with one aim – to maximise pharmaceutical profit margins. There is also the problem with mercury poisoning, immune system overload by use of up to 6 vaccines at once, sudden infant death syndrome, infringement of personal liberty, the fact that most people who get the disease in question have already been vaccinated and that the diseases for which vaccines are required have virtually been eliminated from society.

She attempts to bamboozle her opponent with multiple points at once! Sometimes known as the *'Gish Gallop'*. It can be effective against an inexperienced opponent. It can also allow the topic of debate to be steered into areas where the user has more knowledge.

Frank: I am aware of all these objections, but they have all been invalidated by the CDC.

CDC = Centers for Disease Control and Prevention, USA.

Vera: They would, wouldn't they? I bet the CDC has strong undisclosed links with the

Not a very strong reply. No actual evidence just insinuation pharmaceutical industry.

Frank: So, what process do you think is best to seek out the truth. Are you familiar with epidemiological methods and in particular the principles of a case-control study.

Powerful attack. Frank is guessing she does not know about it.

Vera: I've have heard of it.

Never admit ignorance directly!

Slightly patronising response.

Frank: Basically, you study the incidence of, say, measles over the years and then compare the number of cases of measles in those vaccinated to those who are not. As you know, measles incidence fell dramatically after the introduction of a vaccine in the 1960s.

Vera: I Know that, but at the same time the level of hygiene in Western societies has improved. So, your example proves nothing.

Frank: That's not quite right. Western children who are not vaccinated continue to get the disease whereas those who receive it do not. Also are you aware of the incidence of autism in the UK for example?

Good evidence. Now attacking with detail.

Looking for depth of knowledge.

Vera: It's about 2000 new cases per year.

Good factual knowledge apparently.

Frank: That's right, so by chance you are going to find some kids

Planning to talk about epidemiological principles and

with both. So how would you know that there are more cases than expected if MMR actually was harmful.

Vera: You just count the numbers each year before and after introduction of MMR

trying to catch her out.

She displays ignorance of epidemiological methods. Frank must avoid humiliating.

Frank: Well, it's not so simple as that, as you have to adjust for confounders that may affect autism incidence, like a child's age, socio-economic group, family history etc. Raw numbers can mean very little. Anyway, are you proposing to abolish all compulsory vaccination?

Frank wins the point and now turns to another demolition job. The word 'confounders' is used particularly by epidemiologists to refer to variables such as age, gender, social class etc, all of which need adjustment in the final analysis. He hopes Vera will not be familiar with this specialist word. Now a *change of subject.*

Vera: Precisely, I would abolish all compulsory vaccination for school entry as it interferes with personal liberty and freedom of choice.

Frank: Do parents have the right to deny vaccination for their children?

A *rhetorical question* to which Frank knows the answer.

Vera: Absolutely right, they do

Frank: There is a ruling in many Western countries that a child has a right to the best medical care irrespective of their parents' view.

Correct.

Vera: I don't think parents should inflict dangerous treatment on their children

Frank: That's just the view of the anti-vaxxers that you share, but not the majority opinion voiced by the scientific community. Parents should be guided by the parliamentary democracy in which they live. If the majority in their country have agreed that vaccination for children is in its best interests, then this over-rides the parents view.

Majority opinion is used but not defined. It could mean just 51% of people.

Vera: I think that's plain wrong.

An *ex-cathedra* statement. Just a bold assertion of personal belief not backed up by evidence.

Frank: Well, if every parent took your view there would be no vaccination and a massive amount of childhood illness and death.

Frank is using the '*extreme approach*', similar to Kant ethics.

Vera: I disagree, we now have good herd immunity and there is no need for any more vaccination programmes.

Circular reasoning.

Frank: Only thanks to previous vaccination programmes do we now have a significant level of herd immunity. Are you aware of the effects of visitors from other countries where there is no

Again, a *rhetorical question.*

compulsory vaccination?

Vera: It is my understanding that there is little harm as a result.

It is my understanding – always a weak phrase.

Frank: That's not correct. Visitors for example from Romania, where vaccination uptake is low, have brought in many infectious diseases resulting in small epidemics.

Correct and good point.

Vera: I believe that people should be allowed to suffer infections as and when they arise so that they build up their own immunity, the natural way. If there is sufferance it's for a good reason. Children should be allowed to develop their immune systems without the need for government interference.

Changing the topic. Sort of 'Straw Man' approach.

Frank: Ah! That's the Panglossian fallacy! Surely you don't believe in that?

Few people have heard of the *Panglossian Fallacy*. A concept proposed by Voltaire. See Chapter Two, section on fallacies.

Vera: Never heard of it but I don't take back what I just said. There are thousands of people out there who support my view.

Vera *admits ignorance* – never a good tactic. She also uses the *bandwagon fallacy* here. This could be attacked at some point.

Frank: Even if it results in hundreds of deaths in babies and young children when you know full well that we have the means

The *like with like* argument.

Accusing your opponent of murder will just inflame the debate.

to prevent them? That's like denying antibiotics for someone with pneumonia. Tantamount to murder by proxy! Do you have children of your own?

Vera: No, I don't.

Frank: Perhaps if you did have, you might be more sympathetic to vaccinations. Have you ever seen photos of a deformed baby or a still birth because of rubella (German measles) infection during pregnancy?

Vera: No, never, but I have seen babies with severe seizures and mental retardation that were due to whooping cough vaccine.

Frank: Maybe you should broaden your outlook and perhaps that would make you change your mind.

Lastly Frank is starting to *attack the player not the ball.* Not the best of debating techniques but it often works.

A ruthless question. It will lose friends but could make one's opponent think more deeply.

Correct, but extremely rare. Anecdotal evidence only, but a skilful and quick change of subject.

Ends with a judgemental and emotional stalemate.

13. PRIVATE HEALTH CARE IN UK

Consultant doctors employed by the NHS are allowed to undertake private practice in their spare time – typically evenings and weekends. This may allow a consultant to increase his gross income several-fold – in the case of surgeons, pre-tax income may exceed £1 million. Such practice is undertaken in private hospitals or clinics, or sometimes on NHS premises. Not every doctor is able to engage in private practice because of the nature of their speciality e.g., geriatric medicine or paediatrics whereas, some believe it to be morally wrong. This mock debate is between Toby, a rich consultant orthopaedic surgeon and Harold a reporter.

Cartoon Pt 2.10

Harold: As you are aware, there has been a lot of adverse publicity concerning doctors who often spend too much of their time lining their pockets in the private sector.

Clear statement – although *judgemental* ('lining their pockets').

Toby: I totally agree with the concerns of the public – they are wholly justified - but you do sound a bit left-leaning perhaps?

Toby appears to agree. A powerful and potentially disarming tactic sometimes called *Socratic jujitsu*. Toby tries to *pigeon-hole* his opponent, a useful tactic that implies Harold is just being dogmatic.

Harold: You are heavily involved with private work so why do you continue doing it?

Toby: The private sector exists, and I am contractually allowed to work in it so how can I be accused of doing something wrong? Most of my colleagues would agree that private work provides an important service to busy professional people who may not be able to avail themselves of NHS appointments that often clash with their work.

Initial response is circular reasoning.

'Most of my colleagues' reflects the *bandwagon defence.*

Note emphasis on 'important service' - for whom?

Harold: So, you are really offering preferential service to those who can afford to pay for it i.e. the rich. Surely this is against the principles of the NHS. Should you not spend your spare time offering a better service for your NHS patients.

Straw man attack? The grounds of debate are shifted.

Toby: Well, many of my patients come from less well-off backgrounds and just want a second opinion or a quicker operation than the NHS can provide. I see no wrong in that. I believe I provide a useful service that eases the pressure on long NHS waiting lists.

Toby conveniently omits that he is a major benefactor.

Harold: I believe an NHS patient can get a second opinion within the NHS for the asking but an uninsured patient would rarely be able to afford the fees for you and the hospital for an operation, would they? Can you give me a ball-park figure for say, a hip replacement operation?

'I believe' is a weak statement but probably correct here.

Asking for the cost of a hip operation is a *rhetorical question*, as Harold already knows the answer.

Toby: They vary a lot. You will need to ask one of my colleagues that.

Evasive response. Instead of saying I'm not prepared to answer that.

Harold: Well, I've looked it up on one of the major insurers web pages and they quote a total cost of at least £10,000 of which about half goes to you and the operation takes about 2 hours. Not bad for a day's work – especially if you can do two in one session?

Uncomfortable facts.

Toby: Well, I don't charge quite such high fees, but I certainly know people who charge much more than that. You are paying for several years' surgical experience, of course.

Harold: So how many hip operations in one day would you perform on the NHS?

Laying a trap.

Toby: If things go smoothly, I could probably perform 4-5 as long as my registrar was present.

Harold: So, you are not saying that you are not offering a superior service for the rich and basic care for everyone else? How does that square up with the principles of the NHS and social justice?

Using a *double negative sentence* to try and throw Toby off-guard. *Straw man attack?*

Digging in the knife.

Toby: I think the current hybrid system works quite well as it is.

He would say that wouldn't he?

Harold: OK, so how many days are you away from your base hospital doing private work each week?

Toby: That depends on the time of year, and it varies considerably but typically two whole days and one evening each week.

Once more on the back foot.

Harold: Is it not true that a consultant is contracted to work for 10 sessions per week and if so, you are spending 4 of those sessions in the private sector by day and yet drawing a full-time consultant salary – typically around £140,000 or more.

A consultant who opts for private work must maintain his weekly NHS commitment. Many consultants use 'administration', 'audit' or educational sessions to justify their absence from their base hospital.

Toby: Most of my surgical colleagues work very hard and what we do in our evenings is none of our

Evasive reply.

employers' business.

Harold: So, who looks after your NHS patients when you are absent for those two days?

Attacking the player and not the ball.

Toby: I have some very competent junior staff. If they have a problem, they can call me at any time.

Harold: But these junior staff are there for training as well as service work. How can you oversee their training if you are not there half the time?

Valid but uncomfortable point.

Toby: I've never had a complaint about this.

Evasive reply.

Harold: But don't you write their references? A junior doctor is not going to complain about you, is he?

Even more uncomfortable point.

Toby: I still maintain that the current system although not perfect, works well.

Again, an evasive reply.

Harold: Would you have gone into medicine if there was no private practice?

Attacking the player and not the ball again.

Toby: You're asking me whether I would not have studied medicine? It's just not possible to have a nice house in London and give your children a private education on the basic NHS salary. I know many colleagues who are very happy working full time for the NHS who do no private practice at all.

Repeating the question, useful ploy to buy thinking time. Toby avoids answering the question. *Anecdotal evidence* about colleagues is usually weak and may be attacked easily if you have solid figures.

Harold: No doubt covering for their absent colleagues! Thank you, Toby. Slightly unsavoury conclusion.

14. FREE WILL

This area overlaps with science and philosophy. A religious person will be reluctant to adopt a logical approach and someone who runs out of counter-responses is likely to resort to special pleading, i.e. reliance on personal religious or philosophical beliefs. Related to the concept of 'free will' are the allied issues of 'consciousness' and 'mind'. These terms need to be defined very carefully at the start of any debate to avoid confusion. This mock debate concerns a neuroscientist 'Fred' and a well-read lay person 'Gary'.

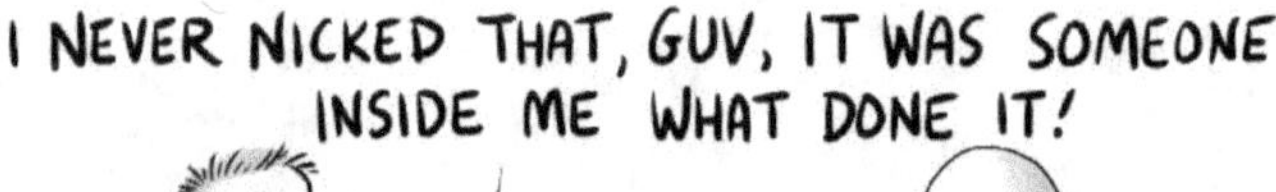

Cartoon Pt 2.11

Fred: You cannot seriously believe that there is such a thing as 'Free Will'. I don't know any neuroscientist who would accept the term.

Aggressive opening stance.

Sweeping and weak statement *'I don't know any'*... The counter argument would be to ask him how many scientists he knows and of these, with how many has he had detailed discussions?

Gary: It really depends on what you mean by 'free will'. For me that implies the ability to come to an independent choice or decision irrespective of past or current events. Most lay people believe that free will exists.

This is just one of many definitions but perfectly acceptable. What *'most people'* believe is a weak tactic – the *bandwagon approach*. There must be evidence, say from surveys.

Fred: so, what's the evidence for your definition?

Asking for evidence is always a powerful means of attack, but in the domain of philosophy there may be little or none.

Gary: If you're asking for scientific trials, I don't know of any, but I do know that I can chose what I want to do.

Weak *anecdotal* response. I know that I can chose, so 'choice must exist' statement is *circular reasoning*.

Fred: Have you heard of the experiments by Benjamin Libet?

Patronising and *rhetorical question*. Now is the time for Gary to keep quiet or change the subject! Maybe use the straw man ploy? Maybe 'throw a dead cat' on the table?

Gary: I believe so.

Never admit complete ignorance even if real.

Fred: Libet was a pioneer in the

The bereitshaftspotential

field of willed behaviour. He asked his subjects to indicate on a special clock face whenever they had the 'urge' to move a finger. At the same time a wave was recorded from the frontal lobes of the brain called the 'bereitshaftspotential' which appears just before any voluntary movement. He found that awareness of the will to move occurred *after* the movement had taken place.

(BP) or 'readiness potential'. If you really wish to humiliate your opponent, then the former would be a preferable term. The BP happens about 350mS (about 1/3rd of a second) before a voluntary movement, but <u>awareness</u> of the will occurs after it.

Use of *low frequency words* is a powerful means of attack.

Gary: Unbelievable.

Fred: Interestingly, he also found that subjects had the power to 'veto' a willed movement up to 200mS before the movement took place. This is sometimes known as 'Free Won't'. Libet concluded that there was no such thing as free will. Many disagreed, but his basic experiments have been repeated and confirmed.

200mS (milliseconds) = one fifth of a second.

Gary: That does not sound like something that is universally agreed and therefore weak evidence. In any case what if it were generally believed that there was no such thing as free will. How would we run society? How would we justify punishment for crime if there was no responsibility?

Reasonable initial point indirectly using the *'divide and rule'* tactic. Thus, if scientists cannot agree, then how can a lay person form an opinion. Gary now draws on the generalisation approach and a slight change of subject – *straw man* defence.

Fred: I agree with you to a point. If we were all robots, it would be difficult to justify punishing people

Good response which ends with a phrase that will *automatically provoke a* for something that they apparently had no control, but there are solutions…

Gary: Well, what are they?

Fred: Do you believe that dogs have free will?

Gary: No, of course not – certainly not in the same way as humans

response that Fred knows he can address. Fred is in control at this point.

Gary takes the bait.

Setting a trap.

This point could be extended to ask at what stage in the evolution of humans was free will acquired.

Fred: Well, everyone knows that you can train a dog by reward and punishment. That being the case, then why cannot a 'robotic' human be trained in the same way? Even if there is free will it is not really needed, is it?

Gary: Well, there's more to life than basic toilet training, eating meals, not barking and so on.

Fred: Agreed, but if you extend the principles from Libet's experiments, the notion that you don't really need free will to modify behaviour then why do some people insist that free will exists? Surely, it's an illusion? Furthermore, is there any evidence, based on the anatomy/physiology/pharmacology of say, the spinal cord, which everyone agrees is an automatically responsive structure, is any

Use of the word 'surely' is weak and makes Fred vulnerable to attack from someone who may ask for evidence. Fred deliberately makes two *longwinded points* in his response. A strategy that can disarm your opponent unless he is concentrating hard. Multiple negatives can have a similar effect.

different *in principle* to the frontal lobes where 'choice' and 'free will' are said to reside?

Gary: I don't know the answer – you're the neuroscientist but my faith tells me you are wrong. Surely, you're not saying humans are basically clever robots?

Concedes defeat in a way and resorts to *'special pleading'* and suspension of reasoned debate. Use of sentence beginning 'surely' is a sign of weakness.

Fred: I take your point and respect that your view is guided by religious preconceptions. However, the only way to resolve this dilemma is by scientific experiment.

Friendly conclusion.

15. VOTING AND ELECTION RIGGING

The right to vote for all citizens above a certain age (excluding prisoners in some countries) is enshrined in the principles of democracy. Despite this, many people do not exercise their right to vote – but why? The following is a mock debate between a libertarian 'Freda' and a well-read left-wing Trade Union member, 'Arthur' who rarely votes. The debate centres around the UK where there are two major parties, Conservative ('Tories'; right wing) and Labour (left wing). Cambridge Analytica is a former UK firm that used thousands of Facebook accounts illegally to create personality profiles and then bombarded those judged to be 'swing' voters with misinformation favouring whoever their investors wanted to win.

Cartoon Pt 2.12

Freda: As you well know, most Western democracies allow all adults with few exceptions, to exercise their right to vote. So why do you not bother?

Arthur: For the most part it's a waste of time. Usually, the outcome is pre-determined by corrupt practice.

Freda: What makes you say that?

Arthur: Well, first of all most newspapers and TV channels are owned by the Tories and all they do is pump out information, true or false, that supports their own party. The rich and powerful, donate huge sums of money to the Tory party – vastly exceeding their Labour rivals. They do this especially before main elections to swing votes in marginal constituencies. Election boundaries are gerrymandered to favour usually a Tory member of parliament and in marginal areas, votes are bought by promising building projects or pledging major facilities such as new hospitals, schools and youth centres, so-called pork-barrel politics. Nearly two thirds of the beneficiaries of the government's £3.6bn Towns Fund in 2019 were marginal seats. Then there's the carpet-

Gentle opening.

Gentle approach – a phrase popular with counsellors!

The '*Gish Gallop*'. Arthur makes multiple points in the hope of swamping his opponent.

Gerrymandering is the practice of moving electoral boundaries to favour one particular political party.

Use of low frequency words may show your intellectual superiority. Same approach with *pork-barrel* and *carpet-bagger.*

A *carpet-bagger* is someone who

baggers who have no local knowledge and come along because of powerful friends, to swing elections. What hope is here against all this? Why is East London such a deprived area – they don't vote Tory of course!

How can it be that the Duke of Westminster owns half of London, and the Church of England owns half the land in England and yet there are still large numbers of homeless beggars in the streets?

Freda: That's a very Marxist approach and you've made some interesting somewhat curmudgeonly points there, but shall we just concentrate on one or two at a time.

What would you like to discuss most?

Arthur: Let's continue with election rigging.

Freda: Surely you don't believe that happens in the UK? What's the evidence?

Arthur: Look – if you've got access to near unlimited funds (as do the Tories) and then early opinion polls suggest that your

lives outside the relevant constituency who is dropped in ('parachuted') to defeat an opponent, either by splitting the vote or actually winning the vote outright.

Arthur steams off the point in mentioning the Duke of Westminster and the Church of England. *Asking yourself questions* is a good strategy that keeps you in control.

Trying to *pigeon-hole* her opponent but with a good calming response which should help focus the debate. Freda hopes Arthur will not know the meaning of the judgemental term *'curmudgeonly'* (bad tempered) and she is probably right as he does not fire back. Low frequency words are a useful means of humiliation.

Use of the term *'surely'* is always a sign of weakness, but asking for evidence is a powerful means of attack.

candidate is losing ground, you can throw money at the problem. You can do more research on the issue, increase advertising, generate persuasive slogans, do more on-site campaigning and supply mis-information through social media. The Labour party's funds come mainly from the Trade Unions which are paltry compared to their opponents' resources.

Freda: That may be the case but what's the evidence for your claims? Also, the electoral commission regulates the amounts of money that can be used before an election.

Again, *asking for evidence* is an excellent means of attack.

Arthur: Well, in 2015 there was a major investigation by the UK Electoral Commission and the police into breaches of spending regulations. It resulted in a fine of £70,000 for the Tories. 20-30 conservatives were investigated for possible criminal conduct and in particular, one person who was found guilty of falsifying election expenses, given a 9-month suspended prison sentence and a £5000 fine. Also, I believe there is a way of donating funds to a local party that bypasses the spending regulations.

All factually correct.

Saying *'I believe there is'* is weak evidence.

Freda: Were any of the other political parties fined?

A *rhetorical question,* - seemingly innocent. This is a powerful tactic, but you must know the answer.

Arthur: I believe that the Labour and Liberal parties were fined small amounts.

Hedged reply.

Freda: Well, it was £20,000 each in fact, so all parties were misbehaving to a degree.

The dagger is plunged, although *two wrongs do not make a right.*

Arthur: True, but the magnitude of fraud was far greater by the Tories and of course there was no re-run of the relevant local elections was there?

Comparing like with like is a useful defence here.

Freda: Have you heard of the issues at the London Borough of Tower Hamlets and the election of the left-wing Lutfur Rahman as Mayor in 2014?

Slight change of subject.

Arthur: I understand there were some problems.

Again, on the back foot.

Freda: Well, there were allegations of double voting, postal vote offences, tampering with ballot papers, intimidation at polling booths etc. that resulted in the deselection of Rahman.

Allegations are not evidence.

Arthur: You have provided good evidence for my stance of not bothering to vote, although I still maintain that most corruption in elections involves the Conservative party. They are just

Avoids responding to the point in question.

Then a further rant! *Gish Gallop* again!

better at covering it up through their 'old boy' network, posh London clubs and massive political funds donated by local fat cats and a fair amount from Russia and China.

Freda: There may be some truth in what you say and I agree a lot is just swept under the carpet.

Appearing to agree is a good strategy and helps keeping the calm!

Arthur: What happens in the UK is no different in principle to the election rigging they say that goes on in many African countries.

Arthur is trying the *'extreme it'* approach.

Use of 'they say' is a sign of weak, or no evidence.

Freda: True to an extent but we do not go around killing or imprisoning our opponents, do we?

Arthur: Sepulveda? Dorkin? Potemkin? Navalny?

Avoids direct response. Changing subject slightly by *blurting out a key name* is a good offensive weapon especially if the opposition has not heard of the name. None of these names apply to the UK.

Freda: Yes, I know about Sepulveda. He's in jail for election rigging in Colombia. He used social media and hacking to influence election results in Colombia, Mexico, and several other central American states.

Unphased by Arthur's attack. She just focuses on Sepulveda. Dorkin was victim of a Russian political assassination. Potemkin refers to a display of empty village building fronts in the time of Catherine the Great. Alexei Navalny was poisoned, recovered, and then put in prison (where he ultimately died) for opposing Putin . In some election

Arthur: Then there is that right-wing hedge fund manager who set up Cambridge Analytica. As you know his firm was implicated in the Brexit, Trump 2016 and Kenyan elections.

Freda: you are right.

Arthur: Going back to your point on assassinations, if the Tory government finds someone who is a nuisance, they would have no hesitation in engaging M15 or MI6 to have them assassinated – just like they did with Princess Diana, Dr David Kelly at the time of the Iraq crisis and the foreign secretary Robin Cook who conveniently died around the same time.

Freda: But that's a far cry from election rigging. Let's leave it there for the moment, shall we?

sites there are physical barriers to conceal manipulation of votes at polling stations.

Good evidence.

Appearing to agree with her opponent once more – but always beware of a trap.

Now a quick return to an earlier subject.

None of these conspiracy theories are proven but they will easily distract. *Mud sticks.*

Peaceful ending?

CONCLUSION

I hope the above will help improve your debating skills and allow you to have fun, as well as victories in argument. Please remember that the examples given above are all hypothetical and do not necessarily reflect my own views. The mock arguments are there primarily to show how some debating techniques may be applied. Also, the numeric data in the mock debates may not be entirely accurate but they should not be too far out.

REFERENCES

Barber BM, Lee YT, Liu YJ, Odean T. *Just how much do individual investors lose by trading?* The Review of Financial Studies. 2009 Feb 1;22(2):609-32.

Bar-Eli M, Azar OH, Ritov I, Keidar-Levin Y, Schein G. *Action bias among elite soccer goalkeepers: The case of penalty kicks. Journal of economic psychology.* 2007 Oct 1;28(5):606-21.

Beckman RC. The Downwave: *Surviving the Second Great Depression.* Dutton Adult; 1983.

Dezhbakhsh H, Rubin PH. *From the 'econometrics of capital punishment' to the 'capital punishment' of econometrics: on the use and abuse of sensitivity analysis. Applied economics.* 2011 Oct 1;43(25):3655-70.

Fagerlin A, Zikmund-Fisher BJ, Ubel PA. *Cure me even if it kills me: preferences for invasive cancer treatment. Medical Decision Making.* 2005 Nov;25(6):614-9.

Gladwell M. The tipping point: *How little things can make a big difference.* Little, Brown; 2006 Nov 1.

Goldacre B. *Bad Pharma: How Drug Companies Mislead Doctors And Harm Patients.* Macmillan; 2014.

Hancock, Jennifer. '*How to Win Arguments Without Arguing: Socratic Jujitsu*' CreateSpace, Independent Publishing Platform. 2017

Heady JA, Morris JN, Kagan A, Raffle PA. *Coronary Heart Disease In London Busmen: A Progress Report With Particular Reference To Physique.* British Journal of Preventive & Social Medicine. 1961 Oct;15(4):143.

Huff D. *How To Lie With Statistics*. WW Norton & Company; 1993 Oct 17.

Kahneman D, Sibony O, Sunstein CR. *Noise: A Flaw In Human Judgment*. Little, Brown; 2021.

Lees K. *Fighting fit? Assessing New Zealand's fiscal sustainability*. New Zealand Institute of Economic Research; 2013 Oct 24.

Levitt SD, Dubner SJ. *Freakonomics*. B ED BOOKS; 2014.

Robson D. *The Intelligence Trap: Revolutionise your Thinking and Make Wiser Decisions*. Hachette UK; 2019.

Rosling Hans. *Factfulness*. Flammarion Press; 2019.

Rusher WA. *How to win arguments*. University Press of America; 1985.

Thaler RH, Sunstein CR. Nudge: *Improving decisions about health, wealth, and happiness*. Penguin Books 2008.

Voltaire, Francois. '*Candide*'. (1759). Penguin classics 2006.

Zimmerman PR. *Statistical variability and the deterrent effect of the death penalty*. American Law and Economics Review. 2009 Oct 1;11(2):370-98.

ABOUT THE AUTHOR

Dr Hawkes is honorary Professor of Neurology, Barts School of Medicine & Dentistry, London and honorary Consultant Neurologist, Barts Health, London. He has a longstanding interest in debating techniques, particularly how and why it is so often abused in the search for truth. He firmly believes that the only way to resolve arguments is through an evidence-based approach and proper application of statistical methods.